The Royal County of Berkshire

by

Luke Over

with illustrations by Michael Bayley
and
photographs by Henry Taunt (c. 1875–90)

The Arms of the County

Published & Printed by Cliveden Press
Priors Way, Bray, Maidenhead, Berkshire SL6 2HP
Tel: Maidenhead (01628) 75151 Fax: (01628) 773090

1995

Copyright © Luke Over, 1995

ISBN 0 9521969 2 1

All rights reserved. No part of this publication may be reproduced, stored in a retrieval system, or transmitted, in any form or by any means, electronic, mechanical, photocopying, recording, or otherwise, without the prior permission of the authors and publisher.

Preface

Berkshire evolved as a county in the ninth century when the Anglo-Saxons created shires from the kingdom of Wessex. Each shire was divided into hundreds, which were notionally 100 hides of land, and these in turn were sub-divided into manors administered by a feudal lord.

Berkshire had 23 hundreds and 192 manors from the outset, with the county town at Wallingford and a developing borough at Reading. All other towns in the county evolved during the medieval period, with the royal tag stemming from the palace at Old Windsor, and the conversion of Windsor Castle into a royal residence from the year 1110.

The county retained its boot-like shape until 1974 when the boundaries were changed. At this time the historic towns of Wallingford, Abingdon and Wantage were lost to Oxfordshire along with the White Horse of Uffington. In exchange Berkshire gained Slough, Eton and other smaller settlements in the east from Buckinghamshire. Further changes are scheduled for 1997 when the county will be administered by six unitary authorities and the county council abolished.

This book does not pretend to be a definitive story of Berkshire or to cover the history of individual settlements in any detail. Hopefully it covers most of the important aspects and outlines the history from prehistoric to modern times.

In researching this book I should like to express my thanks to the Berkshire Library Service, in particular the libraries at Maidenhead and Reading, for making available books and documents as required.

Very special thanks are due to Michael Bayley for his very intricate work in producing the drawings for this book, with reference to his unique historical knowledge.

My thanks also go the Berkshire Archaeological Society for the loan of a series of Henry Taunt photographs taken throughout Berkshire c. 1875–90, and to Dr. G. Astill for permission to reproduce the medieval town maps of Reading, Windsor and Newbury.

With reference to the colour illustrations used on the jacket I should like to acknowledge the Royal Borough of Windsor & Maidenhead for permission to reproduce the painting of Windsor Castle and the Reading Museum Service for the diorama of Reading Abbey and medieval waterfront.

Finally my thanks are due to the publisher Peter Morris and the staff of Cliveden Press and to Veronica Kempton who typed the manuscript.

Luke Over

About the Author

Luke Over studied archaeology in London and has directed and been involved in excavations nationwide and throughout Berkshire for more than 30 years. For the past 20 years he has been the Honorary Secretary of the Berkshire Archaeological Society and is a member of the Berkshire Archaeological Trust Ltd, as well as serving on many national bodies. He is also a vice-president of the Maidenhead Archaeological & Historical Society of which he was an early founder member.

For the past 13 years he has been active as a research historian and a journalist, writing regular historical articles for the *Maidenhead Advertiser* and some national magazines. Following project research he has produced town and church guides and reports on the history of houses, hotels and businesses. He also lectures regularly on history and archaeology as well as travel and natural history.

To date he has written over forty books and booklets on historical subjects including *The Isles of Scilly, Bridport – the evolution of a town, Domesday Revisited*, and the Berkshire section of the *Ordnance Survey Guide to Oxfordshire and Berkshire*. His books on East Berkshire include *The Story of Maidenhead, Maidenhead – a Pictorial History, The Royal Hundred of Bray* and *The Royal Hundred of Cookham*.

Windsor Castle and the Thames (John Kip c. 1725). Note the hayfields on the Eton side of the river.

Contents

	Preface	3
Ch. 1	An Introduction to the County	9
Ch. 2	Stone & Metal	17
Ch. 3	Romano-British Berkshire	27
Ch. 4	Domesday and Before	35
Ch. 5	The Evolution of the Towns	41
Ch. 6	The Early Religious Houses	57
Ch. 7	The Royal Heritage	71
Ch. 8	Development of Town and Countryside	81
Ch. 9	The Golden Fleece	99
Ch. 10	Crime and Punishment	107
Ch. 11	The Civil War	111
Ch. 12	Ancient Sports and Pastimes	119
Ch. 13	Communications, Coaching and Canals	133
Ch. 14	Victorian Expansion and the Railway	143
Ch. 15	The Post-1974 Additions	155
	Unitary Authorities	164
	Index	165

The Royal County of Berkshire

CHAPTER 1
An Introduction to the County

Many of the Home Counties derive their name from the principal or county town as in the case of Buckinghamshire or Oxfordshire. Berkshire is an exception to this rule, which if applied, would have resulted in the county being called Wallingfordshire. The earliest recorded spelling was in the year 860 when it was recorded as Bearrucscir, a name that persisted in that form until 1600.

The Celtic root of the word derives from *barro* meaning "hill", which is present in the form of *berroc* in the writings of the 9th-century monk Asser, who wrote a life of King Alfred. Asser, who was living at the time of its origins, states that the county name comes from what he calls *Berroc silva* (Berroc wood) which he describes as a place where "box grows in great abundance". Experts tend to agree that the wood itself was named after a hill probably situated near Hungerford. Indeed it has been suggested that *Barroc* was originally the name of the Berkshire Downs, an area where King Alfred was born in 849.

The existence of Berroc Wood is supported by a reference to a wood of that name in a charter of King John, dated 1199, confirming to the nuns of Fontévrault the possessions of the nunnery of Amesbury, which had been granted to them in 1179 by Henry II. The location of the wood cannot be determined with certainty but King John's charter mentions Challow, Fawley, South Fawley, Rockley and Letcombe and gives details of rents to be obtained from the wood at *Barroc*. This context suggests that the wood was in the south west of the county, perhaps, as Peake argues, "on the clay lands between and including Enborne and Hungerford". Berkshire's present status as a royal county stems from its

A Longhorn Bull used as draft oxen in Berkshire.

The Berkshire Pig.

The Royal County of Berkshire

association with the royal palace and castle at Windsor.

This book describes the old county before the 1974 boundary changes, and before Wallingford, Wantage and Abingdon, not to mention the White Horse of Uffington, were lost to Oxfordshire in return for Slough and Eton. The old shape of Berkshire was always likened to a football boot, with Windsor on the toe cap and Oxford just across the border at its northernmost extremity. The two towns are linked by the River Thames which formed the northern boundary of the county.

The western boundary follows the route of the River Cole from Buscot to Shrivenham and then crosses the downs from Ashbury to Inkpen. The southern boundary is an arbitary line as it crosses the Eocene sands as far as Sandhurst, where it turns south eastwards on a short stretch back to Windsor. The county abuts Buckinghamshire and Oxfordshire on the north, Wiltshire on the west and Hampshire and Surrey to the south. Buckinghamshire, Middlesex and Surrey can all be seen within the space of one mile if one stands on Runnymede, as King John did when he signed the Magna Carta.

The scenery in Berkshire is perhaps unspectacular, but nevertheless there are many attractive villages nestling among the rolling downs and river valleys. In contrast are the larger towns, all steeped in history and mostly situated on the major waterways. To some extent the pattern of settlement has been determined by the basic geology and topography of the different areas. The solid geology comprises Jurassic, Cretaceous and Eocene bands which run parallel from the west to the east of the county, whilst the river valleys have built up deposits of more recent alluvium.

The oldest deposits are the Jurassic rocks which occur at the north of the county near the top of the boot. The first to occur is the Oxford Clay which rises from the flood plain of the Thames and stretches from Buscot across to North Hinksey. Below this is the Corallian Ridge, a formation of hard limestone running from the Cole to the Thames and embracing villages from Shrivenham to Cumnor. The Vale of the White Horse, a valley carved out by the River Ock, separates the Corallian Ridge from a three mile wide band of Kimmeridge Clay, on which stand Goosey, Denchworth, Drayton and Abingdon.

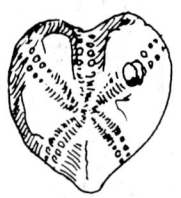

Fossil Sea urchins from the chalk or gravel.

Almshouses at Lyford

The Royal County of Berkshire

After this there is a series of Cretaceous rocks, beginning with a band of gault, which underlies the settlements of Wanborough, Uffington, Steventon and Didcot. An outcrop of Lower Greensand occurring near Faringdon yields some interesting fossils, whilst a band of Upper Greensand runs across from Wantage to Wallingford.

The last of the Cretaceous series is the chalk, which covers one third of the county and forms the basis of the Berkshire Downs. In the west it stretches from Wantage down to the River Kennet, and in the east it covers the area on which Twyford and Maidenhead stand, with an isolated knoll below Windsor Castle. Of the later Eocene clays and sands, the most important of these is the London Clay, which stretches from Inkpen to Bray, and includes the towns of Reading and Newbury. This clay has been used extensively for the production of bricks along its route and played a large part in providing building materials for all major Berkshire towns, replacing the older materials of wood, flint and chalk. The rest of the county on the Hampshire and Surrey borders is a mixture of Reading beds and Bagshot sands, an acid soil not suitable for agriculture, which produces areas of heather, gorse, silver birch and rhododendron.

The county has many waterways, some of which provide drainage for the upland areas. These are described in more detail later but include the rivers Thames, Kennet, Lambourn, Loddon, Blackwater, Pang, Ock and Cole. Many of these provided communication between settlements as did the man made Kennet and Avon Canal, which crossed the county from east to west.

An 18th C. windlass used on Thames flash locks.

Berkshire maintains an intermediate position between London and Bristol, and therefore most main lines of communication crossing the county tended to link these two cities. The earliest is the Roman road, known locally as the Devil's Highway, which crossed the Thames at Staines (*Pontes*) and passed through the south of the county to Silchester (*Calleva Atrebatum*) and then on to Bath (*Aquae Sulis*), where it linked with Bristol. This was replaced later by the Bath Road in the thirteenth century when a river bridge was built across the Thames at Maidenhead. This important coaching route passed through Reading, Newbury and Hungerford before entering Wiltshire. Similarly the railway crossed the county in 1839. All these routes were finally superseded in 1970 when the M4 motorway

The village street at Blewbury

The Royal County of Berkshire

crossed Berkshire like a spinal cord, reducing traffic congestion in many of the main towns.

The post-1974 Berkshire is a much narrower shape, having lost its north-western section, and many of its historic towns. At the eastern end the county has taken on a small part of Buckinghamshire. With the railway and M4 motorway giving quick access to London, the east of the county now serves as a dormitory area for the city and the towns of Maidenhead, Slough, Windsor, Bracknell, Wokingham and Reading are almost adjoined. The whole area is now known as Silicon Valley because of the many hi-tech industries that have sprung up there. Bracknell, one of the largest developed areas, having grown from a small village into a large town over the last 50 years. Meanwhile the downland villages still retain their rural image and are largely unspoilt. Windsor, with its castle, on the River Thames is the top tourist attraction in the county, and helps to reflect its Royal Heritage.

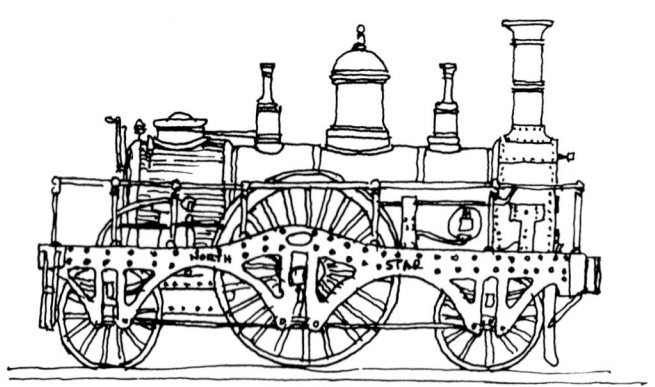

The 'North Star'. First locomotive on the G.W.R.

Berkshire *is bounded on the North by the River Thames, on the South by Hampshire, on the East by Surry, & on the West by Wiltshire & Gloucestershire.*

Reading *the County Town sends 2 Membrs. to Parliamt. Market Sat. Fairs Febru. 2. May 1. Jun. 24. Jul. 25. & Sep. 21.*
Windsor *sends 2 Members to Parliamt. Market Sat. Fairs Jun. 24. Oct. 13. & Easter Tues.*
Abingdon *sends 1. Membr. to Parliamt. Market M. & F. Fairs Jun. 9. Jul. 25. Sept. 2. Nov. 30. a first Mond. in Lent & Mond. after Michaelmas Day.*
Wallingford *sends 2 Members. Market Tu. & F. Fairs Apr. 5. & 25. Jun. 24. Sep. 18. Nov. 1. Dec. 6. Th. before Easter & Whit Mo.*
Maidenhead *Market W. Fairs Jul. 22. Nov. 30. & Whit Wedn.*
Okingham *Market Tuesd. Fairs June 11. Aug. 29. Novr. 2. & Thursd. before Shrove Tide.*
E. Isley *Market W. Fairs Feb. 24. Aug. 15. Easter W. & Whit Wed.*
Newbury *Market Th. Fairs Aug. 24. Oct. 28. Nov. 30. & Holy Thurs.*
Hungerford *Market W. & Fair Aug. 10.*
Wantage *Market S. Fairs July 7. and October 6.*
Lamborn *Market F. Fairs May 1. Sep. 21. Nov. 23. & Whit Monday.*
Faringdon *Market T. Fairs Feb. 2. Aug. 24. Oct. 18. & Whit Tuesday.*

15

The White Horse at Uffington, Britain's oldest hill figure.

CHAPTER 2
Stone and Metal

Evidence of Palaeolithic man, who probably emerged during the last million years, is particularly prolific in Berkshire, although it tends to be confined to the central and eastern parts of the county. The reason for this is that the settlers preferred the larger river valleys and in particular the middle reaches of the Thames.

The existence of Stone Age man is characterized by the assemblage of the stone and bone tools that he left behind. Being principally a nomadic tribe, Palaeolithic man in Berkshire erected flimsy shelters of wood and animal hide, both organic substances which very rarely survived. The settlements of these hunter-gatherers were invariably located on the gravel terraces of a river which afforded both a water supply and a means of communication.

The terraces were formed during the Ice Ages when rivers ran fast or slow according to the amount of ice at the Poles. The Thames Valley, for instance, was carved out to a depth of some 120 feet by fast flowing torrents when the ice was melting, whilst forming a series of flood plains during the times when the river was more stable.

The main surviving tool of Palaeolithic man is the hand-axe fashioned from flint, which has been found in large numbers on the Thames terraces mainly at the east end of the County. The earliest formed terraces are now high above the present flood plain and implements have been found at Toots Farm, Caversham which is at the 114 foot level. Further west finds seem to be confined to three hand-axes located at Upper Basildon.

The Royal County of Berkshire

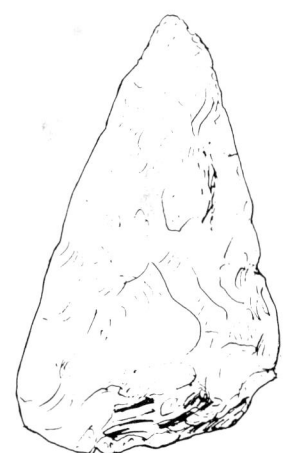

Palaeolithic Handaxe from Maidenhead.

The Royal County of Berkshire

Prehistoric Cereals, Spelt, Emmer.

The stronghold of early Stone Age man in Berkshire seems to have been the Thames terraces in the Maidenhead area where large quantities of axes have been found at Furze Platt, Boyn Hill and Burnham. So prolific were the finds that the terraces stretching the full length of the Thames have been named from sites in this area. After the present flood plain comes the Taplow terrace followed by the Boyn Hill, Lynch Hill, Furze Platt, and Winter Hill terraces. The British Museum has several groups of axes from Kinghorne Pit, Furze Platt, which was excavated in the 19th century but produced axes as recently as 1990. Notable among the early antiquaries were Dr Joseph Stevens who recognized early Stone Age occupation at Grovelands Pit, Reading in 1881, and Llewellyn Treacher who located a large assemblage of implements from the Twyford area, presumably from the gravels of the river Loddon.

In contrast to Palaeolithic man, the people of the Mesolithic or Middle Stone Age appeared to be dependent on fish as the main ingredient of their diet. This does not mean that they did not hunt animals, but with a warmer climate it is likely that in some places forest extended down to the river's edge, making access difficult. Whilst the Thames pick took the place of the earlier handaxe, the main assemblage of tools changed to a series of microliths, much more suitable for the spearing of fish.

Mesolithic man appears to have migrated to Britain from the Continent around 10,000 B.C. and radiocarbon dates from their occupation of Berkshire range from 8415±170 B.C. at Thatcham down to 3310±130 B.C. at Wawcott. Once again settlement was in the river valleys but tended to be confined to smaller rivers, streams and tributaries. Strangely enough the Thames has yielded little or no Mesolithic occupation, but evidence could conceivably be blotted out by alluvium deposits.

The main area of finds has been on the banks of the River Kennet where groups of implements and chipping floors have been excavated. These floors indicate the point of manufacture of the microliths. Finds extend westwards to the River Lambourn and east to Holyport where on the Shafflemoor Stream several thousand flints were located.

One important point emerges from the evidence of Palaeolithic and Mesolithic cultures in Berkshire. Unless research is sadly lacking it would appear that during these periods no apparant use was made of the large areas of downland that occur in the west of the county. It is not until the third stage of the Stone Age that we see any attempt to use the chalklands for any form of agriculture.

The Neolithic people, who were probably operative in Berkshire by 4,000 B.C., brought with them the knowledge of early cereals and animal husbandry. These were the first farmers in Britain and were looking for arable land on which to cultivate their crops of wheat, emmer and spelt. The river valleys were not entirely suitable for their purposes, and therefore we find a spread of occupation up in the chalk downlands, and forest clearance in other areas.

The implements of this period, whilst still made of flint and stone, were much more sophisticated. Axes were smooth and polished and in some cases hafted, whilst flint arrowheads were designed for hunting. Picks fashioned from deer antler were used as a digging tool, and other items were manufactured from bone.

The first pottery was introduced into Britain at this time. It was essentially a very crude ware with round sagging bases which was designed to stand on an open fire when being used for cooking, perhaps some early form of porridge. Decoration, when it occurred, was confined to simple indentations, probably made with a piece of wood. This early pottery was termed Windmill Hill and Grimston/Lyles Hill ware, as identified at British typesites, with the later Peterborough ware occurring after 2000 B.C.

Neolithic occupation sites have been found all over the county, but given that the main building materials were still wood, flint and chalk with no early form of cement, little evidence of their round houses has survived. However, unlike the earlier stages of the Stone Age several types of earthworks have been identified and excavated. The first of these is the henge monument, in the form of a ring ditch, that has mainly been found on the gravels. As at Stonehenge, it has been assumed that these are some form of ritual temple with ditches to keep out the evil spirits.

Stone and Metal

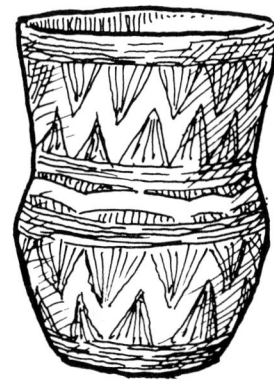

A Bronze Age Beaker.

The Royal County of Berkshire

The much larger causewayed camps comprised a ditch with causeways at intervals which may have been used by the prehistoric people in time of siege. Examples of this type of monument have been found at Abingdon, Eton and Yeoveney Lodge, near Runnymede. There are undoubtedly many more still to be located. More impressive are the chambered long barrows or communal burial mounds of which Berkshire has a few examples. Most chambers have been constructed of wood and therefore have collapsed under the weight of the earthern mound. One of this type which was scientifically excavated at Lambourn produced a radiocarbon date of 3415 ± 130 B.C. Another barrow is known as Wayland's Smithy and is located at Ashbury on the Berkshire Ridgeway. Dating evidence seems to suggest that there is an overlap of Middle and New Stone Age cultures in Berkshire. A Mesolithic date of 3310 ± 130 B.C. for a site in the Kennet valley can be compared with a Neolithic date of 3320 ± 110 B.C. at Cannon Hill, Bray in the west of the County.

The ensuing Bronze Age which began around 1800 B.C. marked the first use of metal in Britain. Whilst stone implements remained in use for some time smiths from the continent brought with them the knowledge of bronze manufacture and revolutionised the range of tools and weapons. These included socketed axes and spearheads, palstaves, knives and swords. Many excellent examples have been dredged from the rivers in the county.

During this period an expansion of settlement seems to have taken place in the chalk downs whilst the river valleys remained popular. Evidence of Bronze Age farms and settlements, however, is scanty and little remains of the circular huts which at one time

Wayland's Smithy – A Neolithic Long Barrow.

Wayland's Smithy – a Neolithic Chamber tomb near Ashbury.

The Royal County of Berkshire

A Flowering Rush.

would have been dotted over the landscape. Casual finds of the more durable metal implements have been numerous, and on occasion smiths' hoards have been located. The main evidence seems to have been an increase in the number of sepulchral monuments.

Burial of the dead was mainly in round barrows or burial mounds, of which the main concentration is in the Lambourn area and north-west Berkshire. The contents of the barrows have mainly been rifled in the 19th century but where intact mounds exist they have been found to contain pottery beakers with remnants of food, weapons, adornments and other personal items for the dead person to use in the next world. Some were interred as inhumations, whilst others were cremated and their remains placed in urns.

Many of the burial mounds occur only as ditches in areas where they have become denuded and been ploughed out. Others still stand to a height of 10 feet and can easily be recognised on the skyline. Most barrows occur on high ground but some small groups like those in Mortimer Common and on Cockmarsh, Cookham are sited on the plateau gravels. The most important group in the County are the Seven Barrows, at Lambourn which are situated in the valley bottom. The name is a misnomer, as the total recognised is nearer forty.

These barrows occur in many shapes and sizes and the different types can be seen at Lambourn. The simplest variety is the Bowl Barrow which comprises a mound only, taking on the appearance of an inverted bowl. In contrast the Bell Barrow is surrounded with a small platform and a ditch. The Disc Barrow is mainly platform and ditch with a small low-lying mound in the centre and is often associated with female burials, whilst the rarer Pond Barrow as the name suggests is seen as a depression in the ground.

The study of land usage, which has mainly been carried out on the chalk uplands of the county, is hampered by the fact that there is little evidence of associated settlement. Celtic fields and field systems have mainly been identified from the air and the farming practices can only be assigned to the late prehistoric period, and not specifically to the Bronze Age or the Iron Age that followed. After 1000 B.C. new waves of settlers from the continent introduced new cultures to Berkshire which included the use of iron in metallurgy.

By what is now probably an outdated chronology, the Iron Age settlers came in three waves, and were mainly identified by their pottery and metal wares. These were the Hallstatt culture from Austria (550–300 B.C.), the La Tene culture from Switzerland (300–150 B.C.) and the Belgae from the Marne Region (150 B.C.–A.D.43). To simplify the chronology the terms A, B, C have been used. Of the first two periods evidence in Berkshire is again sparse, and many of the Iron Age farm complexes are only known from the air. Aerial photography has proved the existence of settlements of huts within circular, subrectangular and banjo-shaped enclosures. Some firmly-dated evidence comes from excavated sites at Rams Hill and Beedon Manor Farm.

Stone and Metal

The best-known visible monuments of the early Iron Age are undoubtedly the hill forts of which Berkshire has many examples. They are usually located on hill tops and consist of a ditch, or several ditches surrounding the summit. The last may have one or two entrances and the interior may be an area of several acres. It is generally thought that the people retired to the forts in time of siege, at which time each bank would have been surmounted by a wooden palisade.

A Belgae Coin featuring a horse like that at Uffington.

There are several examples on the Berkshire Ridgeway, itself a prehistoric trackway leaving the Thames at Goring Gap. These include camps at Blewburton Hill, Badbury, Grimsbury, Segsbury, Caesar's Camp, Finchampstead and the Sinodun Hills at Long Wittenham. One fort situated on the Ridgeway is Uffington Castle, which is adjacent to the oldest hill figure in Britain.

The Sinodun Hills, Long Wittenham, site of an Iron Age Fort.

The Iron Age fort at Blewburton.

Stone and Metal

The White Horse of Uffington is considered to be of early Iron Age origin, perhaps contemporary with the nearby fort. Its purpose is elusive and it is not easily visible from the ground. Recent excavations have shown that the present hill figure may be the last of a long line, and that the horse was fashioned by digging trenches in the hillside and packing them with chalk. Tests on silt has now yielded a date of 1000 B.C. for its original construction.

The White Horse on the Berkshire Yeomanry badge.

The Belgae, who were certainly in southern Britain by 100 B.C., brought with them some new innovations. Well trained in the use of metal, their tools were more sophisticated than the previous settlers. They introduced coinage to Britain, which was based on the Greek silver stater of Philip of Macedon. Numerous examples of their coins have come to light in Berkshire as casual finds. Their pottery was wheel-made superseding the cruder coarse wares of their ancestors. They introduced trading into Britain and excavation has shown that they did business with Roman Gaul. On a Belgic site at Knowl Hill and another at Burghfield parts of Hofheim flagons manufactured by the Romans were found amongst locally-made pottery.

The Belgae often chose settlement sites which were later used by the Romans. This was true at Knowl Hill where a Roman-British villa was erected nearby. They can perhaps also be credited with building the first towns, or oppida, which comprised several acres of buildings on level ground surrounded by a boundary ditch. There are no good examples in Berkshire but the Roman city at Silchester started in this way.

Dragon Hill from Uffington Castle.

An enclosure called Robin Hood's Arbour, Maidenhead Thicket, was excavated in 1959 and proved to be an animal pound of this period. Nearby a semi-circular earthwork is thought to be a boundary ditch of a similar date. These sites date to just before the Roman invasion which was to change the face of the county.

The Royal County of Berkshire

An Iron Age House.

CHAPTER 3
Romano-British Berkshire

The Claudian invasion of A.D. 43 was to change the face of Britain and Berkshire alike. The British were no match for the superior forces of the Roman army and it was not long before the country became the Roman province of *Britannia*. Whilst many did not welcome the new invaders, in time their advanced technology proved to be an asset. After all, the Romans were master builders, having previously set up a network of roads and towns in all their conquered territories. They also brought with them the knowledge of central heating and built shopping precincts and leisure centres, which were not to reappear until the 20th century.

At the time of the invasion Berkshire was in the territory of the Atrebates tribe who were ruled from the Belgic oppidum at Silchester, south of Reading. As with many Belgic towns, which were apparently well sited, the Romans adapted and rebuilt the capital into their administrative centre of *Calleva Atrebatum*. The town was laid out on a grid system within a boundary with the internal roads forming insulae on which town houses and shops were erected. Later the boundary ditch was replaced by a mainly flint wall with four gates, which surrounded the city.

In the centre of the city the Romans created a basilica and forum, forerunners of the modern town hall and market place, whilst in other sections there were temples and inns. The complete layout of the town is known from excavations in the late 19th century and more recent work which started in the 1970s. Finds from all the excavations can be seen in the Silchester Room at Reading Museum. Near the east gate of *Calleva* but outside the wall

Coin of Vespianus 70–79 A.D.

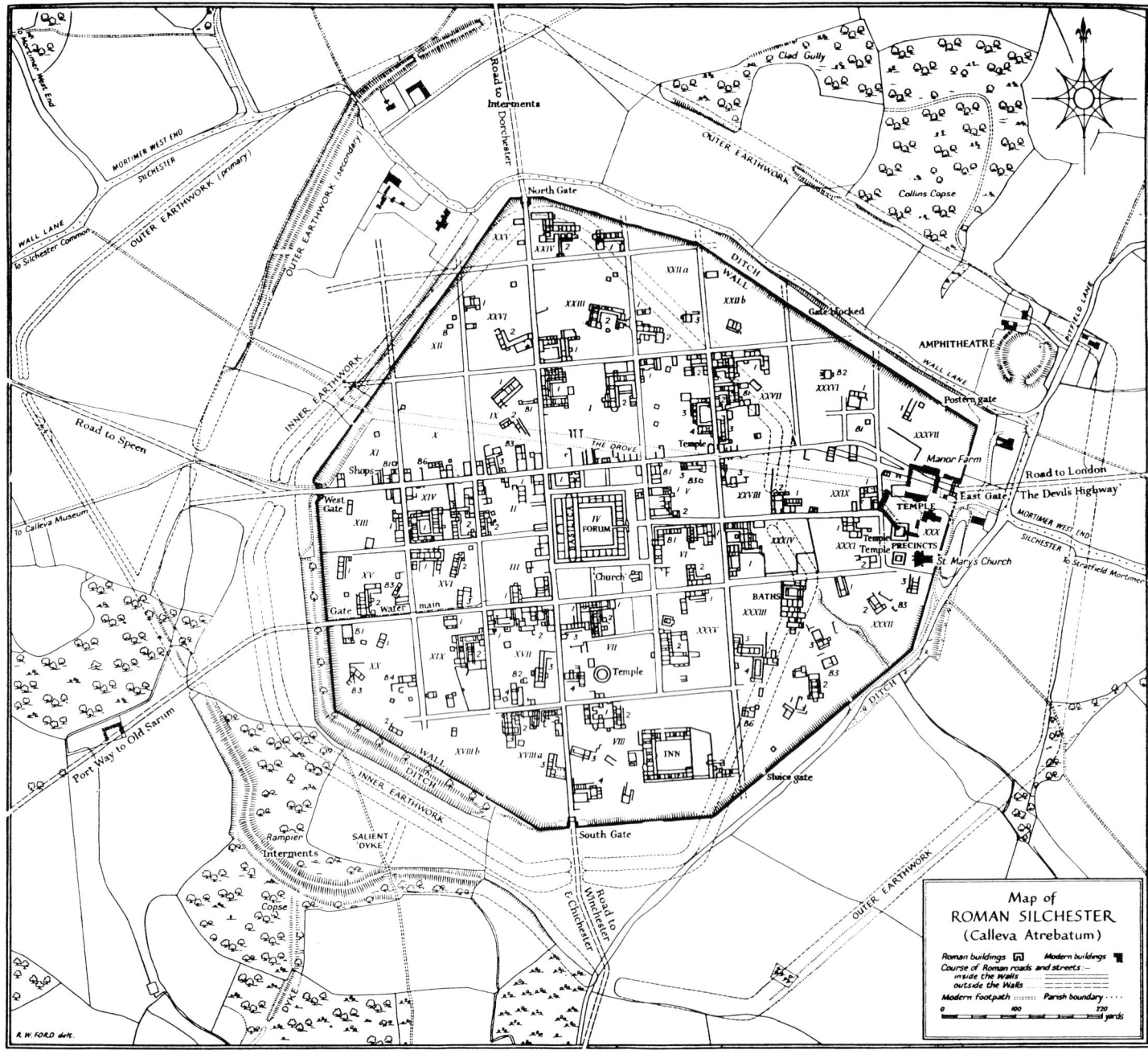

is the amphitheatre used for gladiatorial combat and other entertainments for the citizens.

Tantalisingly the Roman city of *Calleva* is a mile over the county border into Hampshire, but should be mentioned as it can be looked upon as the earliest county town for Berkshire. The other important Roman towns in the area, namely Dorchester-on-Thames, Staines and Mildenhall, Wiltshire are once again just over the border, leaving the county to boast just a few minor settlements.

However, roads linking the main towns are mentioned in the Antonine Itinerary, a Roman document which lists the majority of roads and towns existing in Britain. The first of these was the so-called Devil's Highway, that linked *Londinium*, the capital with the Spa at *Aquae Sulis* (Bath). This passed through Staines, the river crossing of *Pontes*, and crossed the acid soils below Easthampstead en route to *Calleva*. Excavations here show that there was a small settlement at Wickham Bushes, close to the fort at Caesar's Camp. The road is well defined in this area and can be followed over a long distance.

All major roads in the county passed through Silchester and this road continues to the town of *Cunetio* (Mildenhall) in Wilts and then to Bath. Ermine Street also leaves the city in this direction on its way to *Corinium* (Cirencester). It passes through Thatcham, a conjectural Roman settlement, and then to Speen, near Newbury, which may be identified with the wayside settlement *Spinae*. Before leaving the county it passes Wanborough, identified as another settlement.

The road to Dorchester-on-Thames runs north from *Calleva* through Pangbourne crossing the Thames just before reaching its destination. The roads so far described leave a large gap in the system in the north-west of the county indicating rural settlement on the Berkshire Downs. There must, however, have been undiscovered minor roads which linked the rural farms in this area.

A road that is not mentioned in the Itinerary but thought to exist is that linking *Calleva* with the city of *Verulamium* (St Albans), which was the cantonal capital of the Catuvallauni tribe. The road has been traced from St Albans to the Thames at Cookham by

Romano-British Berkshire

Coin of Marcus Aurelius 161–180 A.D.

Roman Coins from Chaddle Hill, Slough.

29

The Royal County of Berkshire

the Viatores, but from there the route is obscure. Straight lines drawn on a map would indicate that the road would pass west of Maidenhead and through Waltham St Lawrence. The discovery of an octagonal Roman temple and other finds at Waltham show that there was probably a Romano-British settlement on the site which could be linked to this road known as the Camlet Way.

Evidence of a bridge and weapons dredged from the river at Cookham indicate the possibility of an inland port on Sashes Island, Cookham. Recent theories suggest that the Romans used the river for transportation of heavy loads on a regular basis, and where a road crossed a river it was an ideal site for loading barges. Such a set-up at Cookham would necessitate a settlement associated with the crossing.

As previously mentioned, with an empire as organised as the Romans, there must also have been a network of minor roads linking the rural areas. One such road has been traced from Bray to Cookham and crosses the Camlet Way at a point where remains have been excavated. The surface of these minor roads is often difficult to locate and are not as prominent as the *agger* or camber of the principal highways. In Berkshire all roads are built from available local materials mainly gravel, flint and chalk, and are sometimes indistinguishable from those built at a later date.

Indications are that the whole County was predominantly a rural area during the Romano-British era, and the lack of military installations seems to emphasise this. With the exception of a few specialised buildings, the main feature seems to be the villa-farm, of which numerous examples have been located. With their normal precision the Roman land surveyors seem to have triangulated the buildings so that they occur at one and a half mile intervals presumably to assure that each villa controls a certain acreage of land and the crops planted thereon. In some cases these villa estates appear to have developed later into medieval manors and modern farms.

Villas in Berkshire normally have up to 10 rooms, and in no way match the much grander examples which one can visit at Chedworth, Bignor or Lullingstone. Berkshire was undoubtedly not a rich area in Roman times and this is reflected by the lack of mosaic

Romano-British Berkshire

floors in examples found throughout the county. Excavations in the Cox Green villa near Maidenhead showed that villas increased in size according to available wealth. The first century example was a simple rectangular building, developing in three stages to a large house with a full suite of baths by the fourth century. These later examples were normally enlarged by adding two wings and a corridor at the back and front of the building.

The construction of villas depended on local available building materials which were mainly flint and chalk bound together with a crude mortar. Roofing was with *imbrex* and *tegula* tiles, which were manufactured specifically for the purpose as were the tesserae used in the paved floors. Beneath the floor of larger villas was often a hypocaust system and furnaces to provide central heating for the buildings. Walls were painted and occasionally decorated with patterns. Apart from the main building there was usually a further complex of structures which included barns, granaries, corn-drying kilns, animal byres and accommodation for the workers on the estate. In some cases the whole complex was surrounded with a wall.

Cox Green Roman Villa, Maidenhead A.D. 200.

The Royal County of Berkshire

Villas were not only occupied by important Roman citizens, but also Romanised Britons of some stature, who saw the advantage of falling in line with the conquerors. Their role would be to administer estates and provide cereals and meat to feed the occupational army as well as the local population. Commodities sold at market would be subject to a local tax to be paid to the Roman overlords at *Calleva*, the cantonal capital.

It is interesting to note that villas are mainly located on the richer soils of the county and the river valleys. Only one possible example has been located on the poorer acid soils near Bracknell. The distribution is mainly in east and central Berkshire within a reasonable distance of Calleva, which would have been the main market centre. Notable examples of villas have been excavated or located at Frilford, Letcombe, Hampstead Norris, Lambourne, Basildon, Littlewick, Cox Green and Maidenhead. At Woolstone, in the White Horse Vale, a building yielded two pavements.

The downland in the west of the county has so far provided little evidence of villa estates: Maddle Farm, where a major building and even drying facilities have been located, may be the only good example. Perhaps the fact that water sources are not readily available has some bearing on the matter; or that the downland was too distant from the market centre. The scanty evidence so far provided seems to show that commodities produced in this area may only have been for purely local consumption.

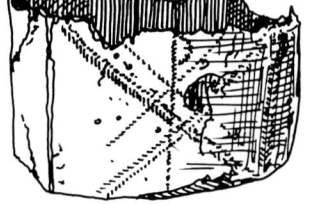

A Roman Font from Caversham.

Evidence of Christianity during the Romano-British occupation is rare in Berkshire. A Christian church is thought to have existed at Silchester, but the only firm evidence comes from Caversham. In 1988 a Roman font was located on a possible villa site at Dean's Farm, Lower Caversham. It emerged from a well as a battered piece of lead, but was found after restoration to be decorated with a 'Chi-Rho' symbol, the first two letters of the name Christ in the Greek alphabet. The font cannot be precisely dated but was in use between 313 and 361, the period during which Christianity was tolerated. Its association with a villa suggests that these buildings may also have assumed the role of the later parish church.

Roman burials in Berkshire, however, have proved to be pagan, as inhumations and some cremations are associated with burial goods and personal items like jewellery. At Bray a

*Romano-British
Berkshire*

*Orpheus Pavement
from a Roman
building at Littlecote.*

33

The Royal County of Berkshire

large cemetery of some hundred skeletons and cremations was excavated in 1972 on the flood plain of the Thames. To date the results of this excavation remain unpublished but evidence of a structure on the edge of the cemetery suggested the possible existence of a Roman hospital.

An analysis of the skeletal remains showed that many of the dead, which included both men and women, had limbs missing which suggested that amputations had taken place. Others had part of their skull cut away, a barbaric ritual performed to release evil spirits. One can imagine that these operations were carried out without pain-killing drugs. Many of the bones showed signs of severe arthritis when examined by experts, although whether this would result in death is a matter of conjecture.

Skeleton from a Roman site at Uffington.

The ashes of cremated corpses were contained in burial urns, which in common with other pottery and finds from the excavation could be dated to the 5th century during the last stages of Roman occupation. The final phases of the site showed signs of metal working and other industrial activity.

Pottery during this period was good quality, wheel-made, and mainly the product of local kilns. The main groups of kilns occur to the north of Slough at Fulmer and Hedgerly. As well as local wares, large quantities were imported both from Dorset and the New Forest and from the continent, the best examples being the Samian ware from France.

CHAPTER 4
Domesday and Before

After the departure of the Romans the comparatively organised communities throughout the county suffered a relapse. Roman villas rotted away or were burnt down by a series of raiders who used the Thames as a highway. This early activity is mainly evidenced from warrior burials and weapons dredged from the rivers, as there are very few cases of wooden buildings surviving. At Moor Farm, Holyport, possible buildings with brushwood floors were excavated in peat, which yielded a date of around 620.

The Anglo-Saxon Chronicle records the dates of many of these early raids notably when Danish ships sailed up the Thames and fought the battle of 'Acleah' in 851, and 870–1 when the Danes held Reading and built the Forbury mound there. In 1006 raiders destroyed Wallingford and for five years, between 1009 and 1013, settlements along the Thames were devastated and part of Oxford was burnt down.

Despite this, Saxon settlement in the Thames Valley was taking place by the fifth century A.D. as evidenced by pottery from Bray. Christianity was brought to the area in 635 when Birinus, a bishop from Rome, established his see at Dorchester-on-Thames and began converting the West Saxons. It follows from this that the majority of burials with grave goods were undoubtedly pagan and earlier than this date, unless they were hurriedly-buried pagan invaders as in the case of a 9th-century burial at Sonning.

Examples of these pagan cemeteries occur mainly on the borders of the Thames. There were two groups in Reading, one near the mouth of the Kennet where 14 burials

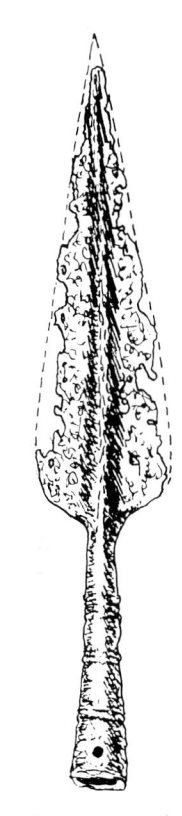

A Saxon spearhead from Slough.

The Royal County of Berkshire

A possible Saxon hound from Bray Chauntrey Chapel.

Alfred, King of Wessex.

were discovered, more than half of which were cremations. The other was alongside the King's Road and yielded 51 inhumations. At Cookham six skeletons together with swords, knives and shield bosses were discovered when the railway was cut in a field called Noah's Ark. Strangely enough, 38 graves were excavated at another area known as Noah's Ark at Frilford, not far from the River Ock. A secondary burial of a warrior was located at Cockmarsh, Cookham, in an existing Bronze Age barrow.

Settlers were once again attracted to the river valleys and evidence in the west of the county is sparse. Fortunately there are a number of charters in documentary form which show that the downland was divided into Saxon estates by the 10th century. The charters for Lambourn and Bucklebury, for example, encompass a large area of the downs.

Berkshire has always been said to be part of the Kingdom of Wessex, although at times it was ruled by the Mercian kings. Be that as it may, King Alfred of Wessex was born in Wantage in 849 and by 892, in response to the Danish invasions, had completed a plan of fortified centres. These 'burhs', as they were known, were listed in the document known as the Burghal Hideage, and included two on the River Thames at Wallingford and Cookham. The earthern banks of the former, which later developed into a town, can still be seen. At Cookham the fort was situated at Sashes Island in the middle of the Thames, and was defended by 1,000 men during times of siege.

Cookham is the subject of three Saxon charters, and with the addition of the fort, must be considered an important frontier town. One charter, dated 798, confirms the existence of a monastery there and a minster. The second, in 975, heralds the beginning of a royal manor and the third, in 996, chronicles a meeting of the Witan under Ethelred the Unready, suggesting the existence of a Royal Palace here.

Other settlements which were of some significance in the 10th century were Bucklebury, which was a royal manor, and Kintbury, which was another royal villa with a minster church. White Waltham similarly had a minster and was the centre of a royal estate and hunting centre. Sonning, on the other hand, was the centre of an ecclesiastical estate and the site of an episcopal residence.

The square at Wantage with Alfred's statue.

The Royal County of Berkshire

The evidence from the Domesday Survey provides us with a lot more information on the layout of the Saxon shire as it was at the time of the Norman Conquest in 1066. Although primarily a Norman document, it gives details of the manors as they were at the time of the takeover and the subsequent changes made by the conquerors. Written in 1086 at the request of William I, the document gives details of all manors in the county. Having said that, the document cannot be used as a gazetteer of sites as there are some discrepancies. Abingdon, for instance, receives no mention as a settlement even though the abbey there owned a large percentage of the county.

For those who know little of the Domesday Book it should be pointed out that the document was compiled primarily so that William I could extract tax from his tenants. Each entry, therefore, gives details of the manor resources, population, ownership and value but may omit details of abbeys and churches and other items which came into the non-taxable category. This, however, does not mean that they did not exist. Similarly some small settlements that exist today receive no mention in the Domesday Book, but at the time were bracketed under the entry for one large manor. The manor of Whistley, now

The Domesday entry for Old Windsor, with Edward the Confessor and William I.

38

Domesday and Before

shrunken to the small settlement of Whistley Green, also included Twyford and Hurst.

Earl Harold ruled the country for four months before perishing at the Battle of Hastings. He had taken over from Edward the Confessor who had a palace at Old Windsor. Although not classified as such in the Survey, Old Windsor must have taken on the status of a town, with so many people dependent on the royal residence for their livelihood. The castle at New Windsor was built around 1070 on land taken from the manor of Clewer, and it was not until the year 1110 when it came into use as a royal palace that any type of town began to develop on the spot.

Wallingford, which had been one of Alfred's *burhs*, had developed into the county town by 1066 and was the centre of administration. The only other borough recorded was Reading, which had urban units of housing and belonged to the king and the Abbot of Battle. Later the town was to expand around the large abbey started in the year 1121. Apart from Windsor, Reading and Wallingford Domesday Book provides evidence of proto-urban settlements at Aldermaston and Thatcham.

The Survey lists 192 manors in Berkshire and the majority of these were rural. A large part of East Berkshire was taken up with the Forest of Windsor which was a hunting area for the Saxon and Norman kings, otherwise the downland and other areas confirmed Saxon estates perhaps based on earlier Roman agricultural units. Manors were self-sufficient, providing their own food and operating their own mills and fisheries with labourers who worked specifically for the lord of the manor.

King Edward the Confessor (from his seal).

Most Saxon landowners were replaced when William I and the Normans came into power. Berkshire was divided fairly equally between the lands held by the king in his own name, the larger monasteries, and the tenants-in-chief, made up of the knights that had assisted William in the invasion of England. The largest landowner, as one might expect, was the king himself, who held 44 manors, whilst the wealthiest of the monastic establishments was Abingdon Abbey, holding 37 manors mainly in the west. The Norman Knight Henry de Ferrers had 22 estates to his credit otherwise the next largest landowner was Miles-Crispin with eight.

A medieval floor tile depicting jousting.

The bridge over the Thames at Wallingford.

CHAPTER 5
The Evolution of the Towns

Wallingford had evolved as an Anglo-Saxon *burh* in the late 9th century and it is recorded that the town was burnt down by the Danes in 1006. By Domesday, however, it had the status of the county town with a mint, a market and a guild merchant. There were 491 houses mentioned in the Survey, eight having been destroyed in the building of the castle. The town had been laid out on a grid system prior to the Conquest but the later castle motte and precincts took up a quarter of the town in the north-eastern corner. The original timber north gate and the 13th-century stone gate that replaced it were found during excavations in the castle precincts.

During civil wars in the reign of Stephen, the castle was held by Brian Fitzcount, and it is likely that two outer ditches were added as further protection to the motte and bailey. From about 1200 to 1385 the castle was used as a royal residence but fell into decay after that time. Within the precincts stood the college and chapel of St Nicholas which was endowed in 1278. In the early 13th century there were no less than eleven parish churches within the town, but today only three survive — St Mary the More, St Peter's and St Leonards.

The north-west quarter of the town was mainly occupied by the Benedictine priory of the Holy Trinity, founded shortly after the Norman Conquest. There was a guildhall with open shops in the centre of the town and separate corn and fish markets. By about 1250 the prosperity of Wallingford was already on the decline and the diversion of the London to Gloucester road through Abingdon in 1416 hastened the demise of the town. By the 16th century it had shrunk to only half its original size, with the castle falling into ruins.

The Royal County of Berkshire

An Edward the Confessor silver penny minted at Wallingford.

The Royal County of Berkshire

With the decline of Wallingford, the town of Abingdon assumed a new importance. Whilst there is no mention of a town there in Domesday Book, one reference records that there were 10 traders living outside the abbey gates, which assumes a settlement dependent on the abbey. The importance of the religious house can be gauged by the large areas of land held at Domesday, with which it had probably been endowed for several centuries, since its foundation in 675 by Hean, a West Saxon nobleman.

Evidence shows that the abbey was substantially rebuilt in the 10th-century after suffering in Danish raids. The town itself was an administrative centre for the Ock Hundred and there are records of meetings of the Councils and the Witans being held there. Throughout the medieval period the urban community stayed under the control of the monks, and the kitchener at the abbey took the profits of the market granted in the early 12th century and the fairs from the middle of the 13th century. There were riots in 1327 when lay persons tried to gain control of the town, but these attempts failed and the abbey stayed in power until the Dissolution.

The early urban settlement seems to have been centred around the minster church of St Helen's. A market-place had been created by the 11th-century, and finds of medieval pottery in localities near the High Street and Broad Street indicate a spread of the settlement. Recent excavations in the vineyard area of the town have located a cemetery and occupation back to the Roman period.

After the Dissolution the town received powers to appoint mayors, bailiffs and burgesses. However, after the decline of the abbey, trade dropped and only picked up again in the 17th century, when hemp and flax were woven and spun in the town.

The county town of Reading owes its importance to the fact that it is centrally placed in Berkshire with excellent communications to London and Oxford. From early times the town was situated on the roads from Oxford to Southampton and from London to Bristol. The town too is on the banks of the rivers Thames and Kennet, and the later Kennet and Avon canal.

A silver penny of Edward I minted at Reading.

The Town Hall and market at Abingdon.

Reading Market Place and St Lawrence's Church.

The town is first documented in the Anglo-Saxon Chronicle in 870–1 and again in 1006, when the Danes wintered there. Domesday references indicate that it had become a town by 1066, a royal borough with an urban community. Furthermore, two coins minted at Reading show that there was a mint operating between 1044 and 1046. These resources suggest that a market centre was created there by Edward the Confessor.

In 1121 Henry I founded the abbey at Reading which gave the town an increased impetus for development. The king endowed the abbey with lands which included the manor and borough of Reading. He also granted permission for a four-day fair and a mint. Henry II and John granted an additional fair and visited the town regularly.

The monastic complex was large and was surrounded by a wall which stretched from the present market-place into the prison grounds. The ruins of the abbey survive today in Forbury Gardens as indeed do the abbey gate, St John's Hospitium and the mill on the Holy Brook. Recent work on the abbey waterfront has revealed a series of wharves on the Kennet, where supplies for the monastery were unloaded.

Of the old churches in Reading, St Mary's in the Butts is probably on the site of the church mentioned at Domesday. It is likely that the early borough was centred around this. Later the market was moved to the gates of the abbey beside the church of St Lawrence, first documented in the 12th century. The parish church of St Giles is also of early medieval origin.

The evolution of the town of Windsor has to be considered in two parts. Firstly, the post-conquest royal settlement at Old Windsor, and secondly the town of New Windsor which developed as a result of the building of the castle. The Domesday entry, as previously discussed, referred to the urban development built to service the royal palace of Edward the Confessor. It was perhaps the next settlement in importance to Wallingford and Reading, and probably acted as a market centre for the rest of the county. At Domesday there is reference to 25 urban buildings and properties belonging to notable members of the king's court.

The Evolution of the Towns

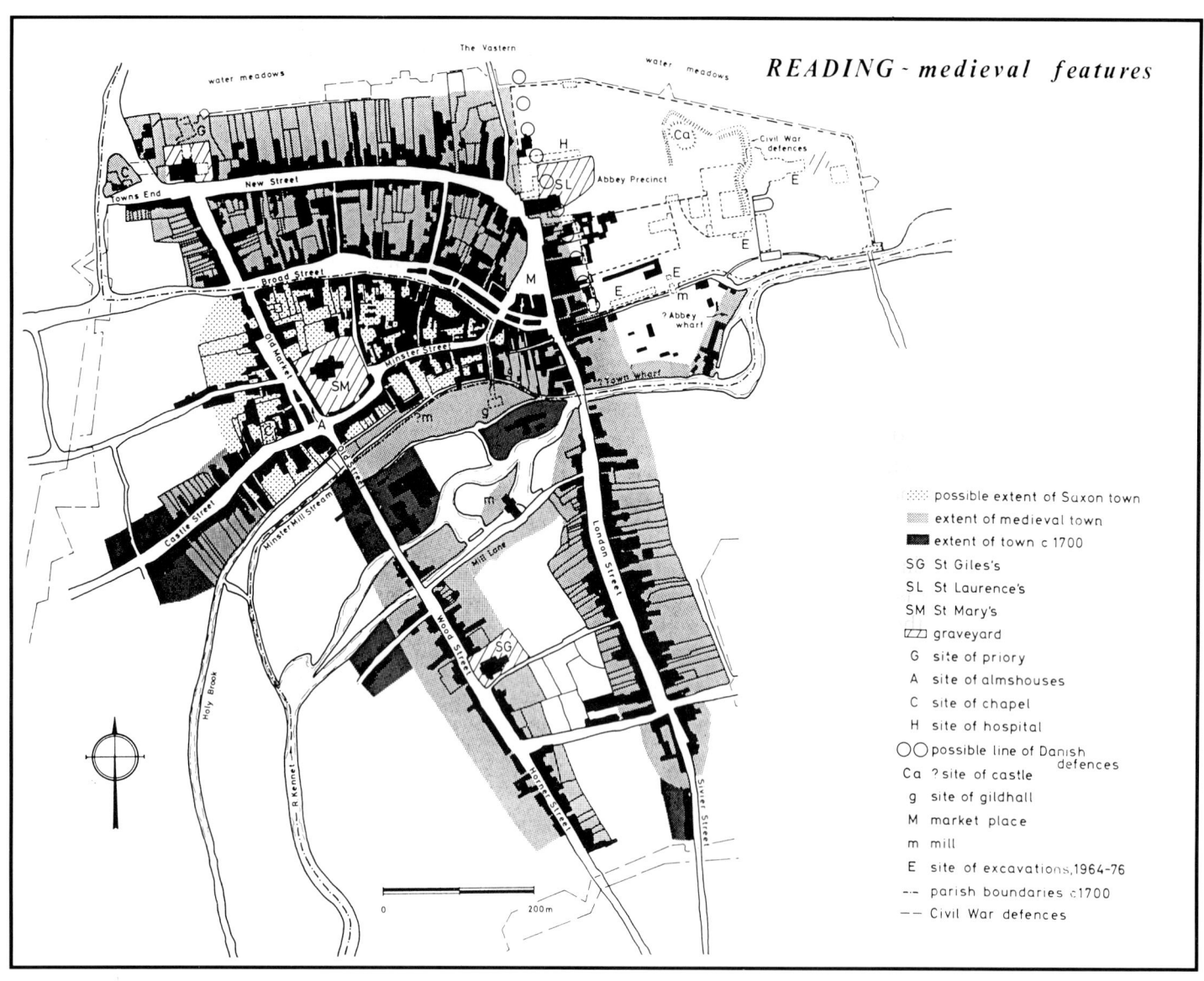

Reading — medieval features.

46

Windsor Castle, was originally built for the defence of the Thames highway, but became the royal residence in 1110 after Henry I had renovated and extended the earthwork. From this date Old Windsor began to decline and the royal palace at Kingsbury fell into ruins. After the siege of the castle in 1216, there are few mentions of the settlement apart from a grange and some associated buildings.

The historic core of New Windsor is clustered around the chalk outcrop overlooking the Thames on which the castle stands. The restricted space available dictated the laying out of Henry I's new settlement. The town grew up around a triangular market-place which faced the main gate of the castle. The parish church, first mentioned in 1184, occupied a central position. From the 12th century, there are several references to a suburb of Underore which grew up below the castle on the banks of the river. It was here that several wharves were erected for barges to unload building materials and provisions for the castle. There was also a ford, which was replaced by a bridge in 1268.

By the late 13th century the suburb of Underore had been linked up with the upper town, and settlement occurred along the streets that had been laid out in between. Further expansion took place along Peascod Street, Sheet Street and Moor Street as the town grew in prosperity. By 1268, in addition to a market and a fair, the town may also have had a merchant guild.

The early inhabitants of New Windsor were totally dependent on the castle for their livelihood. The original stronghold consisted of one motte and two baileys, a layout that still remains. In 1070, wooden palisades stood on the high banks, whilst interior buildings were of timber construction. At the death of Henry II in 1189, the defences of the upper bailey, and the keep had been rebuilt in stone, the lower bailey being completed during the reign of Henry III. The extensive suite of royal apartments was also added at this time, but it was Edward III who transformed the castle into a fortified palace.

The royal parks to the east and south of the town are a survival from the great Forest of Windsor which at one time had a circumference of 77 miles. The forest provided one large hunting ground for the Saxon and Norman kings, and later monarchs, and Windsor was

The Evolution of the Towns

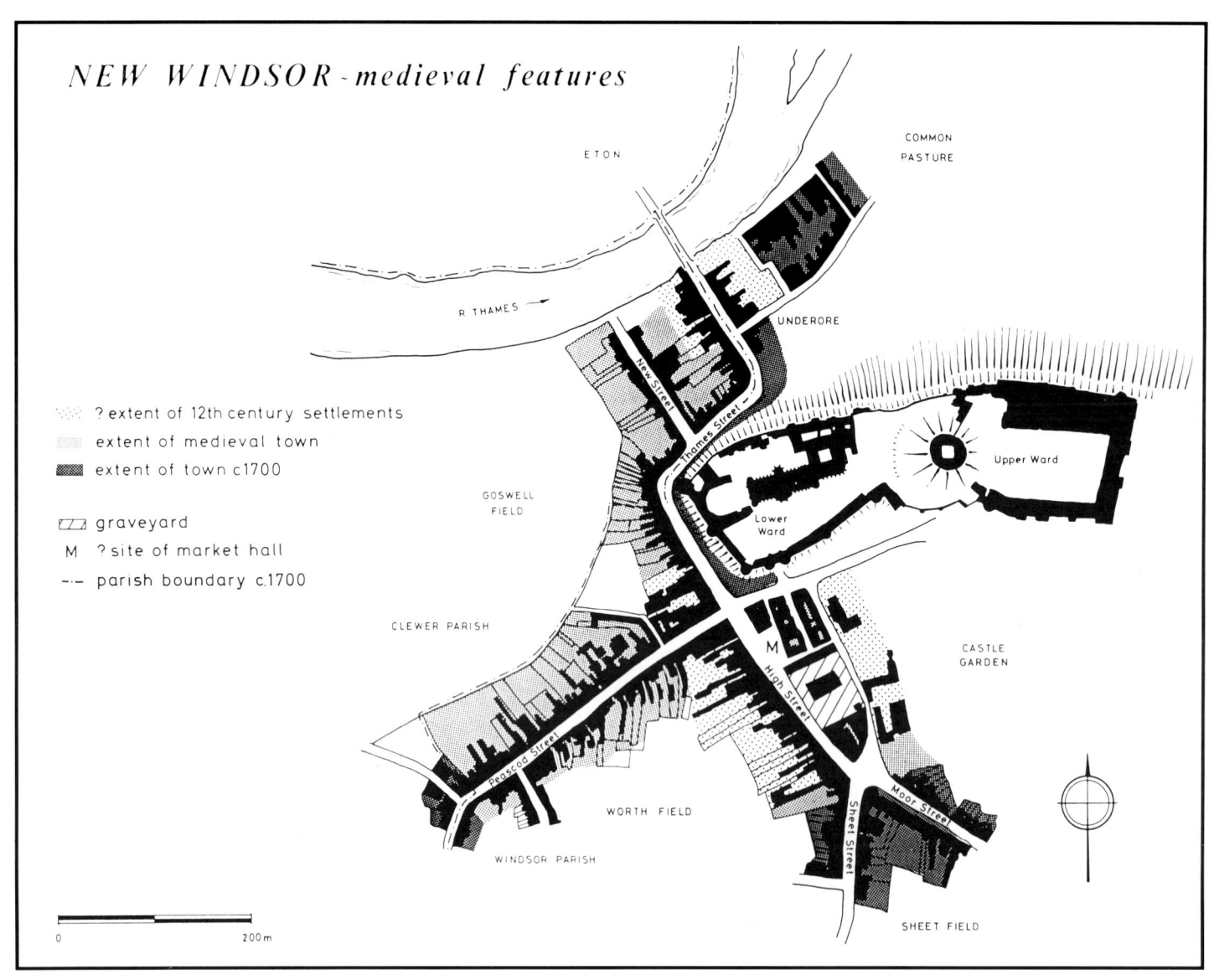

New Windsor— medieval features.

popular for this reason. There were still penalties for anyone found poaching within the confines of the forest, and some were turned out of their homes to make way for the hunted beasts. Hunting lodges were strategically placed to cater for the king and his entourage when out on an expedition.

The town of Maidenhead evolved in the 13th-century as part of the royal manors of Cookham and Bray. The settlement of Elentone to the north of the present town was mentioned in Domesday Book as part of the lands of Giles de Pinkney. Maidenhead was known as South Aylington (Elentone) until the year 1296 when it took on the title of Maidenhythe after the new wharf that had sprung up on the riverside. The town was very much a backwater until the wooden bridge was built across the Thames around 1250, after which it was situated on the main highway from London to Bristol.

The town grew prosperous from the many travellers that passed through and the inhabitants were quick to provide overnight accommodation, stabling, smithies and other trades associated with horse travel. In 1270 a chapel was built at the bottom of the present High Street to cater for residents and travellers alike, and in 1352 this was augmented with a chantry and a separate priest. In 1452, Henry VI granted a licence for the creation of the Guild of St Andrew and St Mary Magdalene whose main responsibility was to maintain the chantry and the bridge.

The wooden bridge was continually falling into disrepair due to heavy traffic. It was the town's lifeline and, therefore, it was necessary to receive gifts of timber from Windsor Forest over a long period. Tolls were collected on the bridge from very early times and a hermit was resident there in 1423. The timber bridge was not replaced until 1777 and tolls continued until 1903.

The medieval settlement, apart from two back lanes, was centred on the High Street from the bottom of Castle Hill to Chapel Arches. It was not felt prudent to continue building closer to the bridge because the area was liable to annual floods. In a way Bridge Street can be regarded as a causeway linking the town and the bridge.

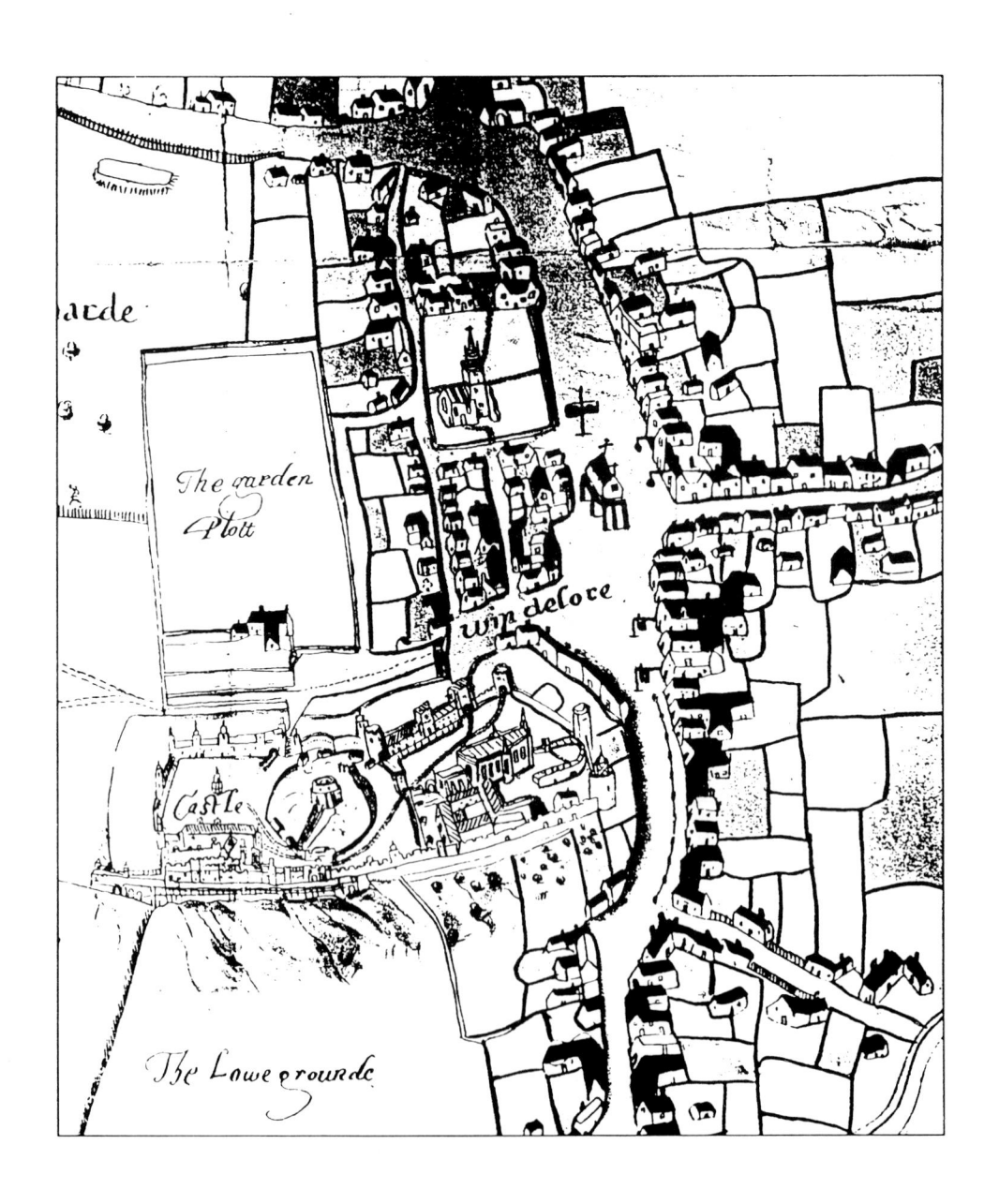

John Norden's map of Windsor c. 1607.

50

The Evolution of the Towns

The origins of Wokingham are a bit of an enigma. Although the place-name is clearly Saxon, heralding the homestead of the people of Wocc', there is virtually no evidence of Saxon activity in the area. The town receives no mention at Domesday and it is assumed that is because it was in a royal forest and therefore not taxable under forest law. There were two settlements, Wokingham Within and Without, the former being part of Sonning under the bishop of Lincoln, and the latter a staging post for the bishop at Sarum.

Wokingham is situated on the acid soils of south-east Berkshire, which was once part of the Windsor Forest; and this is probably why it grew at a later date. The estate is first recorded as part of Sonning in 1146, and a detached part of Wiltshire, which it was until 1845. The town was probably laid out around 1219 when a market was granted, followed by two fairs in 1258. There was no parish church although a chapel was given the right of burial and baptism by 1220. However, All Saints parish church has some 12th-century pier bases in the nave, even if the main arcade dates from the 14th-century.

The original medieval settlement was probably centred around the parish church but eventually spread out along Peach, Rose, Broad and Denmark Streets which encircled the market-place. Wokingham has a fine collection of timber-framed houses in these areas but they are likely to be late medieval.

The other two major towns are at the south-western end of the county on the River Kennet. The first of these is Newbury, notionally the 'new market town', which is mentioned in a grant of 1080 but not recorded at Domesday. It was possibly founded shortly after the Conquest by the Norman lord, Arnulf de Hesdin, who held the last manor at Ulvritone. At Domesday the manor had 51 houses and had increased in value since Saxon times, which indicates that an urban settlement was growing, probably the early town of Newbury.

By 1198 burgesses are mentioned and by 1204 there was a market, fulling mill and corn mill. By 1275 the town had two members of parliament, and representatives attended the king's Council in 1337. The town suffered a decline in the late 13th and 14th centuries, but regained prosperity by the 16th century when the wool and cloth industry was introduced.

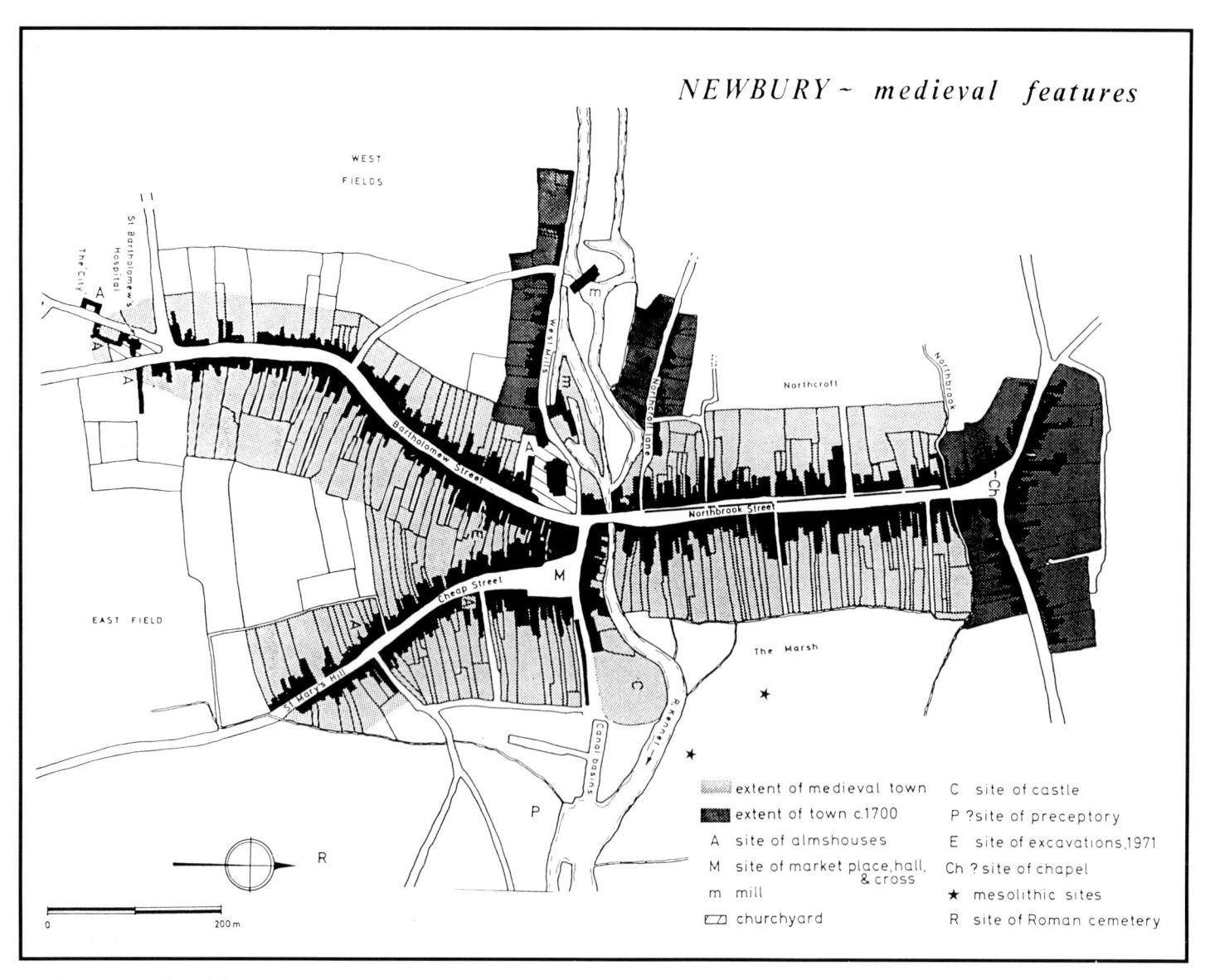

Newbury— medieval features.

The medieval town was laid out in a Y shape surrounding the market, which included Bartholomew, Cheap and Northbrook Streets. The early mills were situated at West Mills. There was originally a castle, mentioned in 1152 when it was stormed by Stephen, but the last reference to the castle site occurs in 1672 when timber was removed from the site to repair the church. The parish church of St Nicholas was built in the 16th century by the cloth merchant John Smallwood, probably on the same site of an earlier church mentioned in 1080.

The second of the Kennet towns is Hungerford, which is thought to have been part of the manor of Kintbury at Domesday. By 1103, however, it is recorded as a separate manor with a parish church. The earliest settlement was probably centred around the church of St Lawrence which now virtually stands in fields to the west of the town. The medieval town seems to have developed each side of the broad High Street perhaps as late as 1200 when a market is mentioned. A town and borough is mentioned in a grant of the manor in 1446.

The Evolution of the Towns

Newbury from the South.

The Royal County of Berkshire

Hungerford had developed into an important market town by the 17th century with two fairs and three markets, for cattle, sheep and wool. There were tanners, saddlers, dyers and weavers in the town who no doubt stood to gain from trading with the rural communities in the downland areas. There were at least two fulling mills on the Kennet to the east of the town.

Four smaller towns which developed little in size after the 18th-century are Aldermaston, Thatcham, Wargrave and Cookham. Today these settlements are classified as large villages, having lost some of their former importance either because of their location or the fact that they were eclipsed by larger towns nearby.

Aldermaston, best known for its atomic establishment, boasted 7 *hagae* in Domesday Book suggesting that the settlement had a proto-urban status. The place-name, meaning 'the farm of the alderman', indicates that it was the centre of a noble estate. It had a minster church and was a royal manor, certainly until 1100 when Henry I granted it to the Achard family. It was a borough by 1298 by which time it had received a grant of a market and fair.

The 12th-century church stands very much on its own but it is likely that the early settlement was grouped around it. The building of a mansion in 1636 and the ultimate extension of Aldermaston Park, first mentioned in 1299, seem to be the reason for the siting of the present village some quarter of a mile north-west of the church.

Thatcham had 12 *hagae* at Domesday and evidence shows that it was a Saxon administrative centre and later the centre of a royal estate and a hundred. It also had a minster church with dependent chapelries at Midgham and Greenham. The manor remained in royal hands unitl 1121 when Henry I gave it to his new abbey at Reading. A market belonging to the abbey was in existence at Thatcham in 1153 and this receives mention again in 1218 when Henry III changed the market day from Sunday to Thursday.

The town became a borough by 1300 but this had ceased to exist by 16th-century. The demise of the town as a market centre was due to the close proximity of Newbury with its thriving industry. An account of 1539 recorded that the market and fair at Thatcham had no value at all.

The Thameside town of Wargrave was the subject of a charter of Edward the Confessor which confirmed a 10th-century grant to the Old Minster of Winchester but this is now considered to be of dubious authenticity. Domesday Book records it as royal manor and it remained in the hands of the Crown until 1189, when it passed to the bishops of Winchester. It was taken back in 1194, but regranted to the bishops in 1199 by King John where it remained until the 16th-century.

In 1218 the town obtained a market charter and in 1225 a borough and hundred of Wargrave is recorded with its own bailiffs and jurors. After the 13th century the market is no longer mentioned and the settlement appears to have diminished from an urban to a rural community. This short lived importance suggests the creation of an early borough on the Winchester estates which was later eclipsed by the town of Henley-on-Thames.

The 11th-century settlement is believed to have been sited near the church on a tributary of the River Loddon. The church, which has a reset 12th-century doorway, was rebuilt in 1914 after an extensive fire, and now stands away from the main town. It would appear that the town was repositioned in the medieval period to take advantage of the road linking Reading with Henley-on-Thames and locations of burgage plots seem to substantiate this.

The importance of Cookham as a Saxon frontier town on the Wessex-Mercian border has previously been mentioned, and a bridge linking Berkshire with Buckinghamshire was not erected until 1840 thus ensuring a good defensive position. In a will of alderman Aelfheah, dated 871, the lands at Cookham passed into royal hands where it remained until 1818. Domesday records it as a royal manor with a 'new market' opened by the Normans, probably at the west-end of the High Street.

The minster church, which has 12th-century features, evolved from the documented 8th-century building, probably destroyed in Viking raids. This church belonged to

The Evolution of the Towns

Martha Spott's token from Cookham.

The Royal County of Berkshire

Reinbald the Priest at Domesday together with lands at Boveney, Binfield and Sunninghill which passed to the Abbey of Cirencester as part of an endowment. The abbot controlled large areas of Cookham land until the dissolution which included pasturage of his animals on the large meadows by the river.

Cookham stands as an area of land liable to flood and whilst the earliest settlement would appear to have centred around the church, the main core of the medieval town was built on each side of the High Street. The 17th-century extension of the settlement occurs at the Pound, which is linked to the High Street by a causeway, and could be very ancient. Like Wargrave, Cookham was given borough status by 1225 but had lost it by 1660. The town lost its early importance when the bridge was built across the Thames at Maidenhead around 1250.

Mapledurham Mill.

CHAPTER 6
The Early Religious Houses

The importance of the abbeys and priories of Berkshire cannot be over-emphasised and therefore some outline of their early history is required. The County is fortunate in having two abbeys of major importance with an early foundation at both Abingdon and Reading, which between them owned large areas of land within Berkshire and as such, to a certain extent, dictated the way of life of their various tenants. These were both Benedictine houses, but there were foundations representing the interests of the Cistercian monks and the Austin Canons amongst others.

Of the houses of Benedictine Monks, Abingdon was by far the most important and richest in Berkshire. It was generally thought to have been founded by Hean, nephew of the chieftain Cissa in the year 675. Hean who with his sister Cilla had resolved to live a life of poverty and humility received a large grant of land and first formed a nunnery dedicated to St Helen at Helenstow, which was later part of Abingdon. This nunnery was later moved to Wytham but was discontinued after a war between Offa and Cynewulf.

The grant of land by Cissa was on condition that a monastery be founded there, and was withdrawn by King Ina when there was a long delay in the building. However, Ina withdrew his objections and the building of the religious house was completed by Hean who became the first abbot. He was succeeded firstly by Cumma and then by Hrethua. The first hundred years were a stormy period for the monastery being close to many local battle sites, including the skirmish between Offa and Cynewulf at Bensington. During this

A Benedictine Monk.

Buildings of Abingdon Abbey.

The Early Religious Houses

period the nunnery at Wytham was disrupted.

The original monastic church, as built by Hean was 120 foot long and had both a western and an eastern apse. There were twelve chambers for the monks with an oratory attached to each. This whole complex was destroyed by the Danes some two hundred years after completion, and its lands were given away by King Alfred who for some reason did not wish to restore the religious house. However, before the middle of the tenth century the monastery was rebuilt by Ethelwold during the reign of King Edgar. He was appointed abbot and was present at the consecration, which took place after 963 when he was appointed Bishop of Winchester.

At the time of the Norman Conquest Ealdred, the seventeenth abbot, was ruling and by 1071 had been removed by King William and imprisoned in the castle at Wallingford. The Norman monk Rainald was in charge at the time of the Domesday Survey in 1086, when it was recorded that the monastery held a large portion of the land in Berkshire as well as a considerable chunk of Oxfordshire with manors in Gloucestershire and Warwickshire.

A charter of Edward the Confessor gave permission to the abbey to hold a market, which proved to be a reasonable source of income. In the twelfth century the market privileges were disputed by the inhabitants of Wallingford and Oxford who, armed with a prohibition order from Henry II, marched on Abingdon and proceeded to clear the market. They were, however, put to flight by the abbot's retainers. The case was further put before the King in Reading who commanded that the weekly market was to continue under the abbey's rule.

The dissolution of the monastery took place on 9th February 1538 when the surrender was signed by the abbot Thomas Rowland, the prior Richard Eynsham and 24 monks. The abbot was given a pension of £200 and allowed to reside in the Cumnor manor house for the rest of his life.

The other large Benedictine abbey in Berkshire was that of Reading of which substantial remains are still extant. Whilst Henry I laid the foundation of the new abbey on 23rd June

A Cistercian Monk.

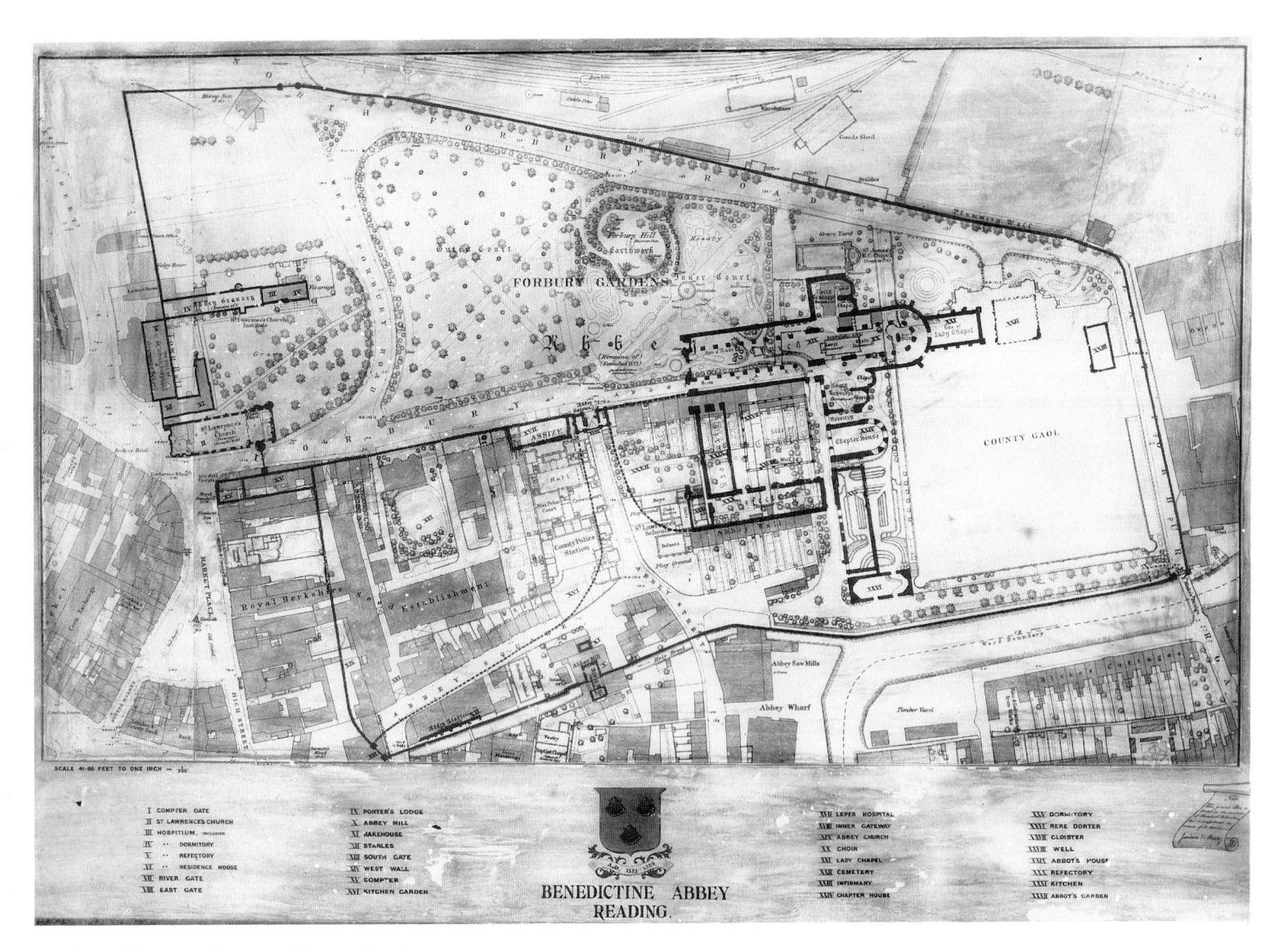

A Plan of the Benedictine Abbey at Reading.

Ruins of Reading Abbey c 1721 & tiles excavated on site.

61

The Royal County of Berkshire

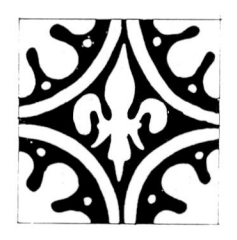

Tiles from Hurley Priory.

1121, it is clear from the foundation charter that there was an earlier abbey there and another at Cholsey which were probably destroyed by the Danes in the year 1006 when they burnt down Wallingford. Cholsey Abbey had been founded in 986 by Ethelred and it is thought that Reading may have been established around the same period.

Be that as it may, Henry I issued a charter in 1125 bestowing on the Abbey lands at Reading, Cholsey and Leominster with churches, woods, mills, fisheries and a mint with one moneyer in Reading. By a series of charters the monks were given immunity from customs, tolls and port dues and jurisdiction over the town of Reading and its precincts. The Abbey was given permission to hold a fair on the festival of St Laurence for four days, and had conferred on them the churches of Thatcham and Wargrave.

The first monks were Cluniacs and the first two abbots members of the Cluniac priory at Lewes, of which Hugo II became abbot in 1199. In 1207 it was still considered to be a Cluniac house but soon after that date became attached to the Benedictine Order.

With the exception of the church, the buildings of the Abbey were completed in five years. Henry I died in December 1135 and his body was interred before the high altar. The great church was completed during the reign of Henry II, and consecrated in 1164 by Archbishop Becket in the presence of the King. By this time the Abbey had been endowed with land at Aston, Stanton Harcourt, Blewbury and East Hendred as well as in other counties. They had also been granted a weekly market at Thatcham and a second fair in Reading on James's day. The hand of St James had been installed in the Abbey as a relic.

Reading Abbey was suppressed in 1539 and the last abbot, Hugh, was hung, drawn and quartered on a platform outside the Abbey gates. The large church, within which many notables and royalty were buried, was allowed to deteriorate until 1548 when the lead was stripped from the roof. Extensive excavations of the Abbey precincts have taken place in the last 30 years and many artifacts are on display in Reading Museum.

The smaller Priory of Hurley came into being in 1086, the year of the Domesday Book. The entry for Hurley mentions the existence of a church but not the Priory which is not unusual as religious houses were not taxable assets. The land and endowments were given by Geoffrey de Mandeville, Earl of Essex, to form a cell of Benedictine monks who were subject to the abbey at Westminster.

The interesting foundation charter states that Geoffrey granted "to God, the church of St Peter of Westminster as also the church of St Mary in Hurley, for the salvation of his soul and that of his wife Leceline and for the soul of Athalais, his first wife and for the souls of his heirs and successors — the church and town and surrounding wood of Hurley, with all rights pertaining, the church of Waltham with a hide and a half of land belonging to it, and the soke of the chapel of Remenham". The church of Waltham is that of Waltham St Lawrence rather than White Waltham, which belonged to the Abbot of Chertsey. There were many witness to this charter including Osmund, Bishop of Sarum, Gilbert, Abbot of Westminster and Aelfric, the builder of the new church of St Mary and of the conventual buildings.

Substantial remains of the Priory still exist today, including the refectory and some barns and a dovecote. The priory church is now shorter than its original size as proved in the excavations of Colonel Rivers-Moore in 1934. Colonel Moore held seances in which he maintained that the powers that be advised him where to dig in order to find buried foundations.

The first recorded prior was Aefric in 1140. The priory received many bequests including land and goods from Essex, Oxford and Ely. Laurence, abbot of Westminster 1159–75 granted to the priory the church of Easthampstead, which was extended to include the whole manor by 1236. In 1397 Pope Boniface confirmed the appropriation of the church of Warfield. The Prior had petitioned for this as at the time the Priory was suffering from the Thames floods and modest endowments, and he claimed royal assistance out of reverence due to Lady Edith, sister of King Edward the Confessor, who was buried at Hurley.

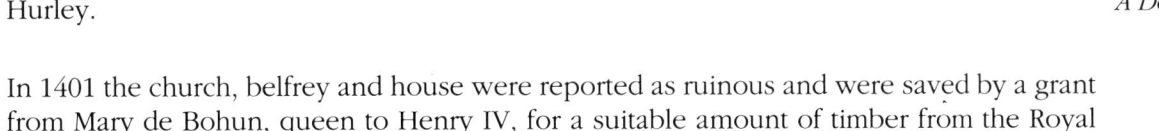

In 1401 the church, belfrey and house were reported as ruinous and were saved by a grant from Mary de Bohun, queen to Henry IV, for a suitable amount of timber from the Royal

The Early Religious Houses

A Dominican or Blackfriar.

Forest. The Priory was again impoverished in 1489 when Richard Lessy came to their rescue with a gift of £60.

The Priory of Hurley was suppressed in 1536 when the manors of Hurley and Easthampstead and the rectories of Hurley, Waltham and Streatley were passed on to Westminster Abbey, which was itself suppressed four years later after which the old priory passed into lay hands.

The foundation of the Benedictine Priory of the Holy Trinity at Wallingford is normally assigned to Robert D'Oyley, a Normal tenant-in-chief who held Wallingford Castle and made substantial gifts at the time of the foundation. However, perhaps the true founder was Paul, the fourteenth abbot of St Albans (1077–93) who sent some of his monks to the church of the Holy Trinity to construct buildings and establish a cell there. Thereafter the history of the Priory is bound up with that of St Albans Abbey up to the Dissolution.

In 1160 Jocelin, Bishop of Salisbury, confirmed "to his beloved and religious sons the monks of St Albans, serving God in the church of the Holy Trinity at Wallingford, all their Berkshire possessions to wit the churches of Holy Trinity, St John, St Martin and St Mary in Wallingford, the church of Hendred, two parts of the tithes of Moulsford, and the whole tithes of the demesnes of Cherseville, Donnington, Earley, Moreton and Sotwell."

The oldest extant charter of the priory is one in the time of Henry I whereby the King granted to the house the tithes of Moulsford and the land of Henry the larderer, with small benefits as they had in the days of King William, his brother, and as on the day when Geoffrey the chamberlain was seised of the land.

In the time when Nicholas of Wallingford was prior, before he was made abbot of Malmsbury in 1182, there was a complaint made about his hospitality. After asking for a nights' lodging a recipient reported that "the prior replied to them with much pride and abusive language, and breaking out in insult, almost to the extent of blows, provoked then by the disgraceful baseness of his words."

Medieval tiles from Cookham.

Dissolution of Wallingford Priory came early after Cardinal Wolsey, commendatory abbot of St Albans, obtained a papal bull in 1524 to dissolve the monastery to provide funds for founding his college in Oxford, but it was not until the 6th July 1528 that the lands and site were transferred by the crown to Wolsey.

Little is known about the early foundation of the Priory of Benedictine Nuns at Bromhall, which was built within the limits of Windsor Forest, the area now known as Sunningdale. The first mention occurs in 1200 when King John bestowed on the priory of St Margaret the church of Sunningwell with all its appurtenances. In 1228 the King ordered Jordan, the forester at Windsor, to give the nuns full access to the 100 acres of waste that he had granted to the Priory, and gave them free pannage for their 36 pigs in 1231. In the same year Henry ordered the Constable of Windsor Castle to grant the prioress timber from the Forest for repairs to the refectory. In 1283 the priory obtained license to enclose the 100 acres of land which they had cultivated with a dyke and hedge which allowed access for deer.

The first recorded prioress was Agnes de St Edmund mentioned in 1268. One of the later prioresses, Juliana Bromhall, was found in 1404 to have appropriated chalices, books, jewels, rents and property for her own use, and was apparently let off lightly as she resigned in the following year. The Priory was destroyed by fire in 1462 along with copies of its early charters. An appeal by the Bishop of Worcester throughout Sarum diocese resulted in a collection being made for a rebuilding programme.

Suppression took place in 1521, at which time the priory comprised a church, mansion, manor, watermill, gate house and gardens. On 21st October 1522 the various possessions were transferred by the crown to the master, fellows and scholars of St John's College, Cambridge.

There were no Cistercian abbeys in Berkshire, but by the foundation charter of the abbey of Beaulieu in Hampshire dated 1204 King John endowed the house with land in the west of the county at Great and Little Faringdon, Great and Little Coxwell, Shilton and Inglesham. At this time a cell was set up in Faringdon whereby a few monks would

The Early Religious Houses

A Franciscan or Greyfriar.

The Royal County of Berkshire

supervise the farming of the property held by Beaulieu.

The Priory of Bisham was perhaps the most important religious house held by the Austin Canons. In the reign of Stephen it had been given by Robert de Ferrers to the Knights Templars but then fell into lay hands. The Austin house was built in 1337 by William Montacute, Earl of Salisbury, and dedicated to Jesus Christ and St Mary the Virgin but this changed later to the Holy Trinity.

The Priory was endowed with land in Somerset and the Isle of Wight as well as the local manors of Bisham and Bulstrode and 104 acres in the parish of Cookham. To this was added the advowson of Curry Rivel, Somerset and Mold in Flintshire. Despite this by 1398 the Bishop of Wells reported that "the priory was weighted down with debt, its rents diminished through pestilence, its church was in the main unbuilt, that its situation of the highway rendered much hospitality necessary, that its arable lands, crops and buildings suffered by the flooding of the Thames, so that the priors' resources were not sufficient for the support of the canons and that of their servants, and for the due discharge of hospitality."

The Priory remained poor until the Dissolution when in July 1537 William the Prior and thirteen monks surrendered. However, the fickle Henry VIII decided to up-grade the house to an abbey providing they prayed for his good health and for the soul of Jane Seymour, his late queen. The new Abbey of the Holy Trinity was endowed with all the property held by the late priory plus the lands from the dissolved abbey of Chertsey and of the priories of Ankerwyke, Little Marlow and Medmenham.

This new foundation lasted only six months due to the erratic demands of the King and on the 19th June 1538 the abbey was dissolved for the second time in a year and was later passed to Henry's wife, Anne of Cleves, as part of a marriage settlement.

Another Austin priory was located at Poughley near Lambourne, and was founded in 1160 by Ralph de Chaddleworth who endowed it with the site of a previous hermitage called "Clenfordmere". The house was dedicated to the honour of St Margaret and assigned to

All Saints Church, Bisham.

Bisham Abbey — a Tudor house on a monastic site.

canons of the order of St Augustine. It was endowed with much land in Berkshire including plots at Faringdon, Colthrop, Lambourn, Peasemore and Speen.

A forty days indulgence was granted by the bishop in 1313, to all who gave assistance to the convent of Poughley, for a grievous fire had destroyed their granaries, mills and other buildings in which their goods were stored. A mill erected in 1428 caused flooding in the adjacent meadows and was the subject of a complaint by John Dyke who held land in the area.

This small priory was amongst the first group of religious houses for the incorporation of which Cardinal Wolsey obtained a pope's bull and the Kings license in 1524, for the use of his college in Oxford. On St Valentine's day, 1525, John Somers, the last prior, surrendered the buildings and the majority of the contents were taken to furnish Wolsey's college.

Another small priory was founded at Sandalford, one mile south of Newbury, between the years 1193 and 1202. It was dedicated to St John the Baptist and endowed with the church and all the lands at Sandalford and a wood at Bradmore. Permission was given to construct a mill on the Enborne and receive 13 marks annually from the mills at Newbury. Information on the history of this priory is scant but it is known that it passed to the collegiate church at Windsor in 1478, when the dean and canons placed a stipendary priest to say divine service at the priory.

The only house of the Hospitallers of St John of Jerusalem was the preceptory at Greenham, in the parish of Thatcham. The house was endowed with the manor of Greenham by Maud, Countess of Clare, and at the same time Gervase Parnell gave them the village. They also acquired the church of Brimpton in the adjoining parish and lands at Shalford, where the hundred rolls of 1276 mentions the Hospitallers of Shalford, perhaps inferring that there was a more important house situated there at the time.

The order of the Hospitallers was suppressed in 1540, and during its temporary restoration under Queen Mary, the preceptory at Greenham was revived with additional endowments. However, when Queen Elizabeth came onto the throne she speedily extinguished it.

Rebra's Well at Crazie's Hill.

Apart from the main religious houses so far mentioned, there were many other smaller foundations. The Franciscans or Grey Friars of Reading were established in the year 1233, and at Donnington, near Newbury, there was a house of Crouched Friars by the year 1404. The County was well supplied with medieval hospitals usually run by the large Benedictine houses for wayfarers and the relief of the sick and aged. These were largely in the main towns and were to be found at Abingdon (3), Childrey, Donnington, Fyfield, Hungerford (2), Lambourne, Newbury (2), Reading (3), Wallingford (2) and Windsor (2).

The County also had three collegiate churches which were situated firstly at Wallingford where it was connected with the Castle, secondly at Windsor with its royal connections and thirdly at the small village of Shottesbrooke; where a complex which included the present parish church was built and endowed in 1337.

Caversham Bridge c 1800, showing the remains of St Anne's Chapel.

The Early Religious Houses

The mill at Streatley.

The Royal County of Berkshire

CHAPTER 7
The Royal Heritage

We cannot be absolutely certain how far back in time the county's royal connections go, but their origins are in the settlement of Old Windsor where a palace was built for the kings which was associated with a royal forest for hunting. Excavations have shown that between the period A.D. 750 and 850 a mill and canal were constructed across a loop in the Thames, but the details of the settlement associated with it are not clear. Documentary evidence, however, records that a royal palace was in existence on the site known as Kingsbury during the reign of Edward the Confessor (1042–1066).

King Edward is recorded as healing the blind in the royal palace of Windsor, and consecrating a new abbot for St Augustine's Abbey in 1061. Just before he died Edward passed the ownership of Windsor to the newly-built Westminster Abbey in January 1066. The grant was subsequently reversed later in the year by William I, who continued to use the royal palace and issued a further charter reading; "By the constitution and favour of the venerable Abbot of Westminster, I have agreed for Windelsora for the King's use, the place appearing proper and convenient for a royal retirement on account of the river and its nearness to the forest for hunting and many other royal conveniences, in exchange for which I have given Wokendune and Feringes". So began the royal connection with Windsor and the County which has lasted to this day.

The Castle at Windsor was at first constructed to guard the Thames Waterway, and was built, on a chalk outcrop belonging to Clewer manor. At this stage there was no town at New Windsor, the settlement at Old Windsor being 1½ miles downstream. The

Soldier of the Royal Berkshire Regiment.

The Royal County of Berkshire

fortification consisted of a defensive ditch, dug around the contours of the hill with wooden palisades mounted on the banks above. The design was a Norman mottle with two baileys, a shape still retained by the modern Castle.

At an early stage some of the timber and wattle structures were replaced by stone, and at Whitsuntide 1110 the Anglo-Saxon Chronicle records that Henry I held his court for the first time in the castle at New Windsor. Henry himself was married in the castle chapel in 1121, and soon after that the Saxon royal residence at Kingsbury went out of use. In the Pipe Rolls of 1130–1 New Windsor is described as a borough, indicating that a degree of settlement had sprung up around the castle.

After the Norman period there were four stages of development in the life of the castle during the Medieval period. In the 12th century, Henry II built a Great Hall in the Lower Ward; and reconstructed the exterior and interior wooden defences in stone, adding the rectangular towers. This occurred between the years 1173 and 1179. In 1230, Henry III, after the castle had been besieged twice, erected a curtain wall with three drum towers on the west side of the fortifications. He also built two separate royal lodgings, one where the present State Apartments are, and another in the Lower Ward. Further to this he erected a large chapel dedicated to Edward the Confessor, which in 1348 became the first St George's Chapel.

The third stage of rebuilding came in the 14th century when Edward III remade the royal residence in the Upper Ward and established a college of secular canons in the Lower Ward with a chapter house for the Order of the Garter services. The final stage was under Edward IV when he started the present St George's Chapel in 1475, which was actually completed in 1528 by King Henry VIII.

During the time of King John the castle underwent two sieges. While Richard Coeur de Lion was on crusade in 1193 his brother John tried to seize the crown and took Windsor Castle. This siege lasted two months after which John's men in the Castle surrendered. Within 20 years the boot was on the other foot. John had travelled to Runnymede to sign the Magna Carta in 1215, which did not satisfy certain of the barons, who with the help of

A Royal Trumpeter.

An early print of Windsor Castle and grounds.

The Royal County of Berkshire

French forces, besieged Windsor Castle in June 1216. John was not present and the Castle was defended by Engelard de Cygony, the Constable, with 60 Knights and footsoldiers. This siege lasted some three months, after which the attackers left Windsor to pursue John's army into East Anglia. The two sieges left the Castle and the town in a sorry state and it was necessary to initiate a rebuilding programme.

After 1216 the Castle had outgrown its use as a medieval fortification and thereafter became a home for the royal family. Additional refinements for the comfort of the monarchs were added after 1239 when Queen Eleanor of Provence gave birth to the future Edward I. During Edward's reign from 1277 to 1307 royal tournaments were held in Windsor Park, and events of this kind soon became a regular feature of life in Windsor. Before 1475, however, Windsor was only one of several royal residences, but after the building of St George's Chapel it acquired a new importance. When Edward IV died in 1483 the new chapel received his body, and Windsor, rather than Westminster Abbey became the traditional burial place of monarchs. Not all were buried there, but the Chapel contains the remains of Henry VIII and Charles I. From 1820, however, members of the royal family have been interred either in St George's, the adjacent Albert Memorial Chapel or in the Royal Mausoleum and its cemetery at nearby Frogmore.

Magna Carta Island, Wraysbury.

During the long reign of Queen Victoria (1837–1901) Windsor took on a new significance. After marrying Prince Albert of Saxe-Coburg in 1840, she spent her first Christmas at the Castle, with what is considered to be the first Christmas tree. Just after her accession she had reviewed the Life Guards, Grenadier Guards and Lancers in the Great Park. The Town, Castle, Borough and Park became the centre for state visits, commencing with the Emperor Nicholas I of Russia in 1844. In the same year King Louis Philippe of France visited and then in 1855 Emperor Napoleon III and the Empress, Eugenie.

Statue of King Alfred born in Wantage in A.D. 849.

The Royal County of Berkshire

Queen Victoria's statue at Windsor.

For the Queen and her visitors there were few gardens that provided privacy and the public stopped their carriages on the main road to Staines to get a glimpse of the royal personages. This was remedied in 1848 when a more circuitous route was constructed one mile to the south. After that Frogmore House and its grounds became a private retreat for the royal family. Before the death of Albert in 1861, the Queen and her Consort had invited a sequence of theatrical performances in the Castle, inventing a new type of social ritual. When Albert died, his bedroom was left unaltered, and was a place of pilgrimage for the Queen. In the Lower Ward of the Castle she reconstructed the Chapel into the Albert Memorial Chapel. The body of her Consort was laid to rest in a special mausoleum at Frogmore, built in the traditions of his homeland.

In 1918 it was found that the foundations of St George's Chapel were giving way. Repairs had been carried out by Sir Christopher Wren in the 1680's, and by Henry Emlyn in the 1770's, but now it needed further restoration. A ten year programme was instigated during which time the foundations were strengthened, new buttresses added, and the nave and choir vaults repaired and replaced. The restored Chapel was re-opened in 1930, and remains the same today with the addition of the memorial chapel to King George VI.

Whilst Queen Victoria had virtually lived in the Castle from 1881 to 1901, King Edward VII preferred to make his home at Buckingham Palace, using Windsor for grand occasions and the large parties for which he was famous. Edward, like his mother before him, valued the Castle as a place for State Visits. Many such visits are recorded including the French President and the King of Portugal in 1903, the Spanish king in 1905, Kaiser Willhelm in 1907 and the Russian Tsar in 1909.

Bombing during the Second World War made it necessary for King George VI and Queen Elizabeth, with Princesses Elizabeth and Margaret to be evacuated to Windsor. Thus our

Eton College's Ten Oared boat on 4th June.

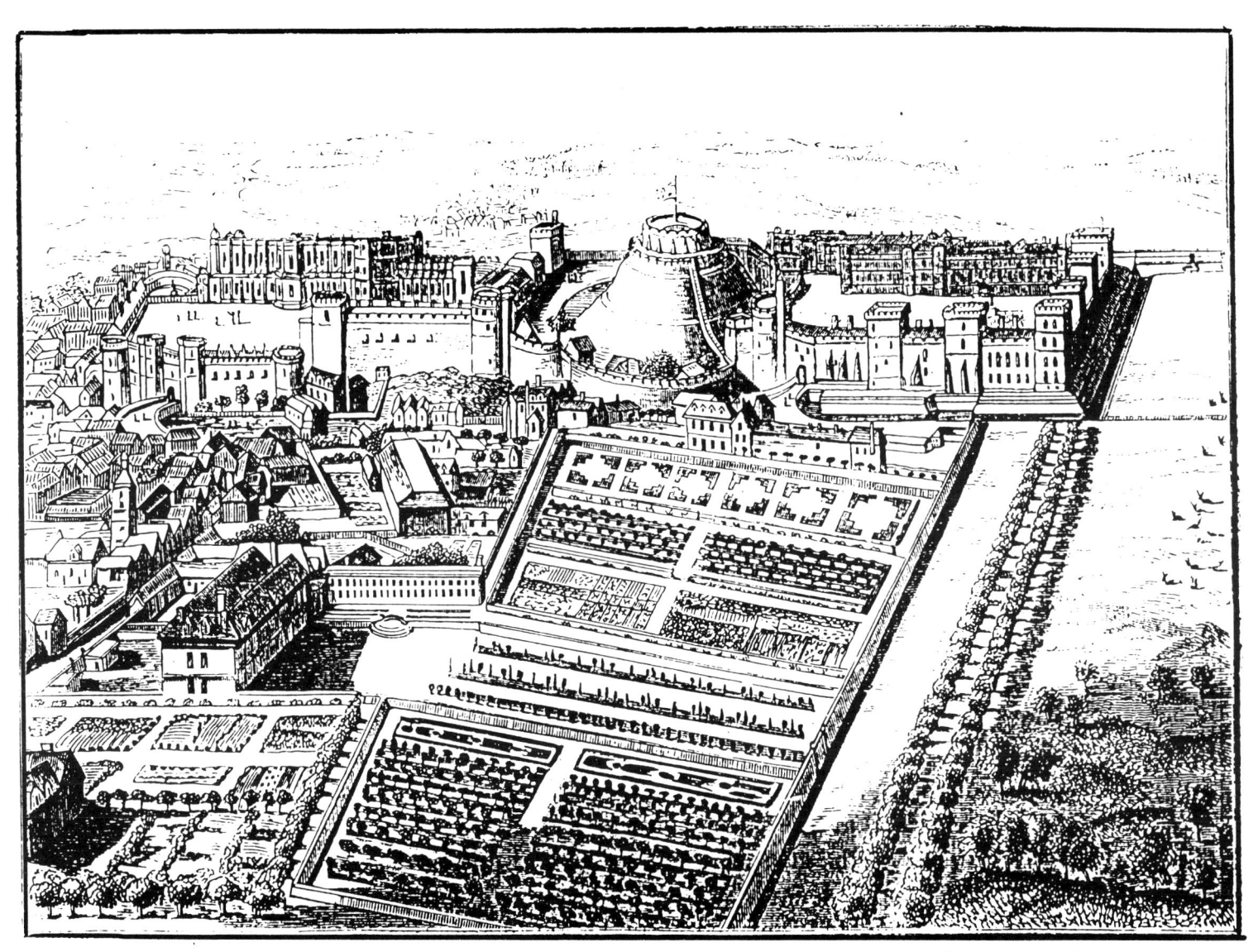

An early print of Windsor Castle and the Thames.

The Royal County of Berkshire

George III on the Copper Horse in Windsor Great Park.

The Royal Military College, Sandhurst.

present Queen was one of the few monarchs, which included Edward III and Edward VI, to be brought up at Windsor. The Town and Castle, as she has often stated, are dear to her heart and she invariably spends Easter, Christmas and Royal Ascot Week there with her family.

Today Windsor and its Castle are one of Britain's major attractions for tourists, and it is seldom that a day passes without the population being increased by visitors from all over the world. It remains part of the county's Royal Heritage, and will hopefully remain so for many centuries to come.

The Swan Hotel at East Ilsley.

London Street, Reading.

CHAPTER 8
Development of Town and Countryside

During the reign of Elizabeth I Reading was still very small and compact and set within a triangle of Friar, Silver and Southampton Streets. The busiest part of the town was to the north of the Kennet where houses were huddled together in dark narrow streets. Names like Hosiers' Lane, Fish Row and Butcher's Row indicated the principal trades that were carried out here. On the eastern side of the market place was Shoemaker's Row, while Gutter Lane was the area with the slaughter houses. The town wharf was to the east of High Bridge and it was here that goods were unloaded and carried to the market stalls.

At the west end of High Bridge was the Guildhall, or Yieldhall, which before the dissolution had accommodated guild members. In the market place were situated the stocks and pillory where many an offender suffered public ridicule. Close by was the prison, known as the Counter, which had formerly been the Abbot's prison. There were seven bridges across the Kennet during this period and these were mentioned as being in need of repair in the Elizabethan charter of 1560, which confirmed an earlier charter of Henry VIII granting the town a Saturday market and four fairs each year.

By now the abbey was in ruins and the principal buildings in the town were the parish churches of St Laurence's, St Mary's and St Giles. Queen Elizabeth is believed to have promoted a new industry of silk weaving in the town by the gift of some mulberry trees. This industry continued well into the 18th century.

The Royal County of Berkshire

During Elizabeth's reign responsibility for the poor of Reading became a major problem. The Abbey and the Grey Friars had provided for them before the dissolution, but the state had not foreseen the legacy that occurred as a result of the suppression of the religious houses. Hoping the matter would go away they passed an Act of Parliament in 1572, transferring the responsibility back to the local parishes. Accordingly the Reading Council converted the former Greyfriars church into a combined hospital and workhouse, but this was only a temporary solution to the problem. With the decline of the wealthy clothing industry increased unemployment boosted the numbers of the poor and the situation grew worse.

As if to make amends for this wealthy clothier John Kendrick left bequests in 1624 of £7,500 to Reading and £4,000 to Newbury which was to be used for providing houses "fit and commodious for setting of the poor on work therein, with a fair garden adjoining". At Reading this resulted in the opening of the Oracle in Minster Street in 1628.

The Town Hall at Abingdon.

Windsor was a town that had reached its medieval extent by the later 13th century, and developed little until the 17th century. Any development taking place tended to fall in line with events at the castle. In 1277 a charter of Edward I created a free borough with burgesses, a merchant guild with freedom of tolls and a county gaol. The location of the College of St George and the Order of the Garter under Edward III did not result in an expansion of the town, and by 1438 there was a noted fall in population. A second borough charter, granted by Henry VI in 1439, attempted to correct the situation by offering financial relief from dues and tolls.

Development of Town and Countryside

Whilst the castle provided a stimulus for both the birth and the continuance of the town, development was stunted by the activities of the royal residents who claimed the town's common lands to enlarge the park surrounding the castle. In the 1460's Edward IV emparked 200 acres of land to which the citizens had common pasture and quarry rights. In compensation for this the King granted a charter of incorporation in 1466 and an additional fair.

The market of the medieval town was sited outside the main fort at the castle, and to some extent retains the same layout today. The present Market Street was once Butcher's Row and Church Street was once Fish Street, showing localisation of trade as in Reading. The old Priest Street was renamed St Albans Street, after the Duke of St Albans, the illegitimate son of Nell Gwynne and Charles II. The town extended along Peascod Street, High Street, Moor Street, Sheet Street and down Thames Street to a ford across the river which was replaced by the bridge leading to Eton in 1236. The Guildhall, standing adjacent to the market was designed between 1686 and 1689 by St Thomas Fitz, and completed by Sir Christopher Wren.

Wokingham Church.

Maidenhead grew very little from its size in 1270 until the year 1835 when the population was still under 800. Throughout this period it continued to cater for those travelling the route to Bristol. The bridge across the Thames proved to be the lifeline for the town and it was necessary at all times to keep it in good repair. In 1452 the Guild of St Andrew and St Mary Magdalene was formed and was charged with the maintenance of the Chauntry in the town and the perpetual repairs to the bridge. During the medieval period the town was still under the control of the royal manors of Cookham and Bray and cases were heard in the manor courts.

The Royal County of Berkshire

A Scene at Hungerford.

Like all religious institutions the Guild was dissolved in 1547 leaving Maidenhead without any corporate control. After thirty years Sir Henry Neville and others made application to Elizabeth I for the re-establishment of a guild or corporation which resulted in the town's first Charter of Incorporation in the year 1582. The Charter made Maidenhead a free town and stated that 'the inhabitants of the said town, and successors thereafter, may and shall be one body corporate and politic in deed, fact and name by the name of the warden, bridgemasters, burgesses and commonality of the town of Maydenheth in the county of Berks'.

The charter provided for a new scale of tolls for merchandise passing over the bridge and for a fishery fifty feet each side of the structure. A grant was made for a market to take place each Monday, and for a Court of Pie Powder to be held during the time of fairs and markets. The market was situated centrally in the High Street at the junction with Market Street where the road outside the Guildhall was wider than it is today. Apart from the market Maidenhead remained 'a street of inns' as described by one early antiquary, with the High Street as its main artury.

One little known event that took place in Maidenhead, probably at the Greyhound Inn, sealed the fate of Sir Walter Raleigh. The evidence comes from a letter written by Sir Thomas Edmondes to the Earl of Shrewsbury. In it he writes: "The Judges have of late met at Maidenhead to consider the crimes of the prisoners; and I understand, they make no question of finding them culpable, save only Sir Walter Raleigh against whom it is said that the proofs are not so pregnant…"

This secret meeting of judges took place in September 1603 two months before the official trial where all the conspirators were found guilty of treason. The reason for holding this witch hunt outside the metropolis was because London had a plague epidemic in the autumn of 1603 in which thirty thousand died. Raleigh was imprisoned and eventually executed in 1618.

After its initial start the town of Newbury suffered a decline in the 13th and 14th centuries, but during the 15th and 16th centuries became prosperous as a wool and cloth producing town, when the industry was controlled by important mercantile families — the Dolmans, the Blandys and John Smallwood, alias 'Jack of Newbury'. In 1596 the town renewed its Charter of Incorporation and a governing body of 31 burgesses were appointed representing clothiers, mercers, tanners, braziers and cloth workers.

A Scene at Newbury.

Kintbury was once the centre of a royal estate. The Norman church is a much restored 12th century structure. However, the churchyard bears witness to earlier occupation with the early Saxon coins and skeletons that have been unearthed there. A charter of the 10th century in existence tells of how Wulfgar left his lands at Inkpen, two miles to the south, to his wife Aeffe. The large parish stretches along both sides of the Kennet, and from Norman times there have been mills there for tanning and wool-dyeing. In the 18th century a silk factory was founded and in more recent years whiting for shoes was manufactured from chalk.

The chalk downs of Berkshire occupy a third of the county in the area to the north west. The whole area is decidedly rural in contrast to the eastern end, and comprises a host of small villages many of which have changed little since medieval times. The biggest settlements are Lambourn, Wantage and Faringdon. Wantage is famous as the birthplace of King Alfred in A.D. 849. He was the youngest of the four sons of Ethelwulf and was crowned King in 871. A fine statue of him stands in the centre of the market place, which was presented to the town by Baron Wantage VC and unveiled by Edward, Prince of Wales, in 1877.

The Royal County of Berkshire

The town of Lambourn is the largest settlement in the Downs and the area is famous for its horse racing activities with many stables. The town is first documented in the Will of King Alfred c. 888 and may have then been the site of a royal residence. The unusually large size of the parish has prompted the suggestion that it was an important Saxon estate which dwindled during the medieval era. A market was probably in existence by 1227 but this had lapsed by 1446 when a new market and two fairs were granted. It seems likely that the town was too inaccessible as an effective marketing centre, and although a new market and fair were again founded in 1669, this had gone by 1870.

A church is mentioned at Lambourn at Domesday and a charter of c. 1090. The present church has a late 12th century tower and nave, was extended in the 13th century and suffered the usual Victorian restoration in 1849.

There is little now to see of the Saxon period in Wantage, which is a town of red brick Georgian buildings, erected around the Market Square. The large cruciform church mainly dates from the 14th century and contains a brass of Sir Ivor Fitz Warin, whose daughter married Dick Whittington, Lord Mayor of London. Its importance as a sheep marketing town is probably illustrated by the entrance passage to the 17th century Stiles almshouses, which is made up of cobbles from the Knucklebones of sheep. The King Alfred Grammar School in Parkway was built in 1850, but incorporates a Norman doorway from the Chapel of St Mary, built by Ethelwulf.

Faringdon is another medium sized market town which had regular sheep markets fed from the farms of the downland settlements. It is at the extreme north west corner of the County and was a royal manor until 1204 when King John endowed it to the newly founded Abbey at Beaulieu in Hampshire. The town has a history of royal allegiance, and during the Civil War the church lost its steeple to the cannon balls of the opposing army.

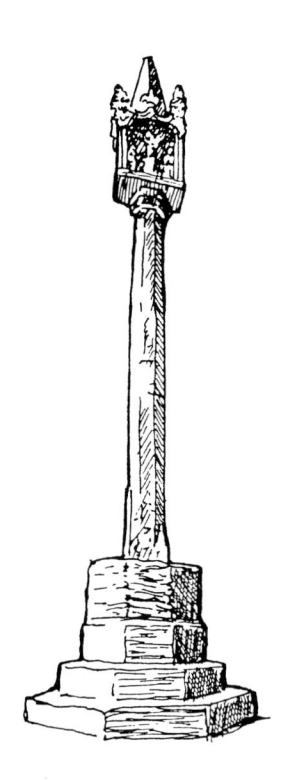

Lambourne Market Cross.

Faringdon is the only Berkshire town with buildings largely made of stone because of its proximity to the Cotswolds. The quaint old market house is well worth seeing as is the fascinating church which has many memorials. The Pye family is well represented. Henry Pye was Poet Laureate from 1799 to 1813, although it is said that he was not very talented.

The Pyes built Faringdon House. On the outskirts of the town is a large Gothic tower, built by Lord Berners in 1934 and said to be the last folly erected in England.

Many of the downland villages are situated each side of the Ridgeway and in the Vale of the White Horse. Most of them were dependent on Wantage, Faringdon and Lambourn for the marketing of the products. The villages are numerous and can only be mentioned briefly. At the western end of Coleshill an ancient moat marks the site of the manor house, whilst Coleshill House was built in 1659 by Sir George Pratt. The village of Great Coxwell, situated on the Corallian beds is famous for its 14th century tythe barn, built by the monks of Beaulieu and reported to be the finest in England.

The settlement of Shrivenham on the road from Faringdon to Swindon has a 12th century church worth a mention. Compton Beauchamp is a parish on the greensand to the west of the Ridgeway where stands Compton House, a 16th century moated grange, featured in Tom Brown's Schooldays.

Uffington, in the Vale below the White Horse, has a church dating to c. 1150 and is where Thomas Hughes spent his childhood. East and West Challow were ancient settlements associated with the Letcombes. Letcombe Bassett is situated at the head of a deep combe, whilst Letcombe Regis was land held by the Crown in antiquity, and had an ancient moated house. The villages of Sparsholt, Childrey and Kingston Lisle are situated on the Port Way, the latter settlement having a blowing stone usually associated with Alfred.

To the north Shillingford has a 13th century church, and near Stanford in the Vale are traces of a mansion at Stanford Farm. The village of Goosey is mentioned in the Abingdon Chronicles as being given to the Abbey by King Offa. West Hannay village

Development of Town and Countryside

St Michael's Church, Lambourn.

Berkshire Fill the Wain.

The Royal County of Berkshire

St Mary's Church, Aldworth.

Long Wittenham Market Cross.

surrounds an ancient stone cross, whilst East Hannay has some interesting timbered cottages with overhanging upper storeys. Steventon has a good selection of half timbered houses along a mile long paved causeway. East Hendred is one of the county's most picturesque villages and has an early 15th century chapel of Jesus of Bethlehem. During the 15th century a weekly market with cloth fairs took place on the 'Golden Mile'. Hendred House is the residence of the Eyston family. East Hendred has changed little since medieval times and its houses are most attractive, as at West Hendred.

The village of Ardington has a church dating from c. 1200 and Ardington House was built in 1721. The settlement of West Ilsley is a village in a hollow with Grimsdyke and the Icknield Way to the north, while East Lockinge is a modern model village built in 1860 by Lord Wantage. The church is in the park of Lockinge House, erected in 1750. Didcot has been mentioned as a junction of the GWR, but the neigbouring village of Harwell is of ancient origin, even if it is now better known as the site of Britain's first nuclear research station. To the north, Drayton lies within a triangle of ancient tracks and Milton House was designed by Inigo Jones in the 18th century.

Sutton Courtney has a fine selection of medieval buildings including a Norman Hall dating to the 12th century. Long Wittenham, which lies below the Sinadun Hills, has a church with a 12th century fort and piscina. Upton is a scattered settlement with some examples of wattle and daub buildings. At nearby Blewbury there is an ancient moat at the Farm House; whilst Aston Tirrold has a Queen Anne manor house and Brightwell a moated site and the remnants of a Norman castle.

Farnborough is situated on the old road running from Hungerford to Abingdon, and has the stump of a medieval cross and a 12th century church. Bright Waltham, also has an early church and a moated manor house, whilst the settlement at Chaddleworth surrounds its church on the top of a hill. Close by is the site of the 13th century Poughley Priory. Wickham, situated on Ermine Street, is the site of a Roman station, and Chieveley, to the east, lies on the ancient route from Oxford to Southampton, and is mentioned in Saxon documents of A.D. 951.

The village of East Hendred in the downs.

The railway halt at East Garston.

The church and village at East Hagbourne.

The Chequers Inn, Charney Bassett.

Development of Town and Countryside

East Ilsley, also on the Southampton Road was an important market town in the middle ages when several roads and downland tracks led to the village, where at times 80 thousand sheep per day were auctioned at the market. The village is in a hollow with the church situated on higher ground. Hampstead Norris, which straddles the river Pang, and its neighbour Yattendon, have connections with the De La Beche family who were manorial lords until 1365. Bucklebury, a Saxon settlement, is said to be the site of the country residence of the Abbots of Reading, and there are abbey fishponds a quarter of a mile from the church.

Despite the fact that the county was named after a wood, the evidence in the Domesday Book shows that in 1086 Berkshire was one of the least wooded shires.

The woodland listed in the survey is measured by the number of pigs, feeding on acorns and beechmast, that it could support over the period of one season. This method of calculation, adopted by the Domesday Commissioners, is of little help when trying to calculate the actual measurements of a particular wood and is frustrating when one finds that in adjoining counties woodland is measured in leagues and can therefore be appreciated in mathematical terms. The number of animals of each category are also listed, whereas they are omitted from the Berkshire entries.

A clay pipe.

At the time of Domesday the extent of the Forest was probably confined to the Windsor district, even though the original hunting ground of the Saxon kings may well have been enlarged. There are records of William I extending the forest and the chronicles of Abingdon Abbey tells of how at Winkfield he turned the 'abodes of men into habitation of beasts'. Under later Norman kings the Forest grew to a vast extent and covered a very large area. It not only included the majority of south east Berkshire as far as Hungerford but it intruded into Bucks, Middlesex and in Surrey along the Wey river as far as Guildford.

The extent of the Forest is again recorded after a great storm in the year 1222 when trees were blown down all over the county. In the forest of Berkshire Henry de Suningewell and Robert de Coleshull were appointed sales commissioners with the job of assessing the damage and selling off the fallen timber. This occurred in January 1223 when it was stated

The Royal County of Berkshire

that Windsor Forest was in the three counties of Berks, Surrey and Hants. In February 1225 a perambulation took place in accordance with the Forest Charter in all these counties to decide which parts were to remain as forest. The commissioners who were appointed for Berkshire were Roger de Cuserug, Jordan the forester and Robert Achard. As a result of this all Berkshire was disafforested except for the Windsor district.

A good idea of the extent of the Berkshire division of Windsor Forest occurs in the years 1498–9 when a list of woodwards was issued. At this time a forest woodward was an important official who was totally responsible for the timber and undergrowth in his charge, as well as the deer that inhabited his area. Most of the woods were actually in private hands but the owners could not, without the King's permission, clear undergrowth, fell timber, erect buildings, establish forges or burn charcoal. They also had to allow access for the King's deer or game, and each woodward, privately appointed, had to take oath before a forest justice to serve the King in the matter of venison, and to present offenders for punishment.

There were 19 woodwards listed in 1498, which indicates the owners and woodwards together with the respective woods.

The Wells Hotel, Sunningwell.

John Halfacre, woodward of Reginald Bray, of his wood called Clewer wood; Robert Bysshop, woodward of the queen, of her wood called Bray Wood; John Lovejoye, woodward of the abbot of Abingdon, of his wood called Wynkefield and Harlewyk wood; Thomas Hodde, woodward of William Nores, knight, of his wood called Burley Busshe; Andrew Wynch, woodward of the queen, of her wood called Altewood; John Ewste, woodward of the queen, of her wood called Bray Wood; Robert Nores, woodward of the prior of Hurley, of his wood called Hurley Wood; Thomas Clers, woodward of the prior of Bisham, of his wood called Bisham Woods; William Skynner, woodward of the king, of his wood called Ashruge; John Fulks, woodward of the abbot of Abingdon, of his wood called

94

Windsor Forest in 1550 (John Speed).

The Royal County of Berkshire

Hirstenhalderst; Nicholas Redych, woodward of the queen of her wood called Benfield; William Mattynglee, woodward of the abbot of Chertsey, of his wood called Lytell Wykewood; Thomas Strode, woodward of Edward Trussell, of his wood called Shortesbroke; Arthur Kemys, woodward of the king, of his wood called Rempneham Wood; John Penvey, woodward of the abbot of Waltham Holy Cross, of his wood called Heywode; Thomas Fennyng, woodward of William Nores, knight, of his wood called Thyket and Knyghtlo; Richard Warner, woodward of the queen, of her wood called Inwood and Bigfrith; John Shepherd, woodward of the bishop of Winchester, of his wood called Wargrave and Waltham; Nicholas Morewode, woodward of John Parkyns, of his wood called Fynchamsted Wood; and Simon Turnor, woodward of William Capell, knight, of his wood called Farleymore.

In the medieval period, the woods and forests of Berkshire were an important economical source. At a time when houses, bridges and other erections were built of timber, large quantities of trees needed to be felled for the purpose. There are many records of grants from the Kings of oaks and other hardened trees for the hasty repairs of bridges which because of the weight of traffic were continually falling down. As well as the aforementioned pigs woodland also supported large herds of deer, which provided a continual source of venison meat, and provided cover for game birds. These resources, especially in forests belonging to the Crown, were jealously guarded and any poaching or breech of other harassing forest laws could be punishable by death.

The parks around Windsor are what is left of the original Forest. The Home Park, which adjoins the Castle is about 400 acres in size and four miles in circumference. There is no stock of deer mainly because it is divided up into gardens and enclosures and offers little cover. Here stood the celebrated Herne's Oak, immortalised by Shakespeare, which fell in August 1863, and was replaced by another in the September by Queen Victoria.

The Great Park contains 1800 acres of land and is fourteen miles in circumference. It is still believed to be stocked with 1000 head of fallow and 100 red deer, whilst the enclosed Cranbourne Park had a small herd of the rarer white red deer. The importance of deer as a source of venison meat, is again illustrated by the number of deer parks that existed

Development of Town and Countryside

throughout the County. The largest of these was at Englefield Park, an area of 450 acres with upwards of 300 fallow deer. When the estate was forfeited to the Crown in 1564, Queen Elizabeth gave the manor to Sir Francis Walsingham, and herself hunted in the park.

Hampstead Marshall Park, which belonged to the Earl of Craven, is another deer park that existed during the reign of Elizabeth, when it was in the hands of Sir Thomas Parry, treasurer of the royal household. The park, which was enlarged in 1665, is around 446 acres and is stocked with 200 fallow deer.

At Hall Place, Hurley, the estate of 160 acres usually has a herd of up to 120 fallow deer. A similar amount can be found at Aldermaston Court, where a deer park of 125 acres is part of a much larger estate. Woolley Park, which was enclosed towards the end of the 18th century, has a maximum of 200 fallow deer in an area of 120 acres. Another 200 may be found at Calcot Park, west of Reading, on the Blagrove estate in which 250 of its 1800 acres are wooded. Other deer parks can be seen at Buckland House (60 acres), Silwood (100), Welford House (200) and Sunninghill Park (250 acres), which was stated in 1818 to be free of tithe as long as 16 head of deer were kept there.

Despite development throughout the County, Berkshire still has many areas of unspoiled wooded parkland. In addition to the numerous estates remaining from the original Windsor Forest, there are some fine parks in the valley of the Kennet notably Coley Park, Prospect Park, Sulhamstead Park, Padworth, Wasing

The Drovers of Coldash.

The Royal County of Berkshire

Place, Woolhampton House, Beenham House and Midgham House. In the Newbury area are Sandalford Priory, Donnington Grove, Benham Park, Hungerford Park and Arlington Manor.

In the far north west of the County are Ashdown Park, Beckett House, Coleshill House and Buscot Park with Lockinge Park, Kingston Lisle Park and the 700 acre Wytham Wood.

JAMES ELLIMAN of SLOUGH

CHAPTER 9
The Golden Fleece

Berkshire has never ranked highly as an important centre for industry, or at least not until the present century when trading estates and business parks have sprung up at Slough, Reading and the east of the County. Before the coming of the railway and the building of the M4 motorway, allowing faster methods of communication, there was little to commend the County as an industrial centre. Such trades that existed were mainly to provide local needs, both from a supply point of view and a source of work for the inhabitants.

The natural resources of the county were not favourable to the growth of any particular activity other than agriculture. However, with farming goes animal husbandry and the extensive range of chalk downland in the west provided excellent foundations for a flourishing cloth industry within the shire. The importance of this industry has now faded, but in Ashmole's time the county was said to have supplied the nation with high quality wares.

Descendant of the Berkshire Nott sheep.

Unlike other counties, the Domesday entry for Berkshire does not list the number of animals, therefore, it is difficult to say how popular sheep farming was in the eleventh century. At a later date, however, we do find large flocks to the west of the County. The Berkshire Nott, now extinct, was said to be a breed which provided excellent fleeces which commanded a high price at the market. It was an animal of large size, with a black face and a large tail, which flourished in folds on the low and cold lands where other breeds failed. Other breeds common in the county were Leicesters, Southdowns, Cotswolds and Wiltshires. In 1792 George III introduced the Spanish or merino sheep with

The Royal County of Berkshire

A Shepherd's Rod.

great expectations but by this time wool from abroad was proving plentiful.

The main sheep breeding district was that between Reading and Wantage, and many villages as with Ilsley and Faringdon held sheep fairs and markets. The regular supply of wool lead to a very healthy cloth industry which during the Tudor period was at its peak. Newbury, Reading and Abingdon were the principal centres and provided work for the townsfolk and other neighbouring villages.

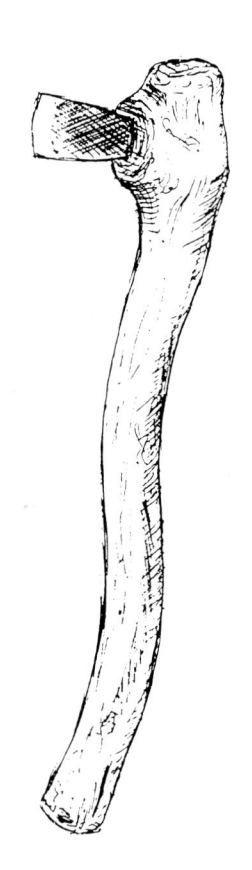

The earliest date for the industry in Berkshire is probably not known and a story that Henry I requested to be buried in Reading "near his good clothiers", cannot be regarded as evidence of the existence of the trade at that time. There is, however, a lot of evidence for early fulling mills and there is one mentioned at Newbury in the year 1205. The Domesday Book records numerous mills along all main rivers including the Thames and the Kennet, of which most at the outset were undoubtedly for producing flour, but may have been rebuilt as fulling mills at a later date.

The Abbot of Abingdon had a fulling mill which was said to be in ruins in 1555, and was waiting to be rebuilt. There was another mill at Westbrooke, near Newbury, in the time of Henry VI, when one Robert Curteys was lessee of a messuage with a fulling mill in Benham Manor. In 1614 Thomas Holmes, of Avington, held Dun Mill at Hungerford which was described as a 'tucking' or fulling mill. The object of the fulling mill, of course, was to make the material shrink and thicken, by saturating the cloth with hot water, and then putting it under the full weight of fulling stocks.

The wool from Berkshire was of such good quality that it commanded a high price on the market, and in 1454 ranked as thirteenth in a list of 44 wools. In the 14th and 15th centuries the County ceased to be pure agricultural, and produced wools for export to the Netherland cloth makers. Meanwhile the cloth industry was expanding in Berkshire and the product of the looms was receiving attention from markets all over the world. In 1549 the English envoy at Antwerp advised Protector Somerset to send to that city for sale a thousand pieces of 'Winchcombe's Kersies'. These were products of the famous Jack of Newbury who figures prominently in the Berkshire clothing industry.

The sheep market at Faringdon.

The sheep fair at East Ilsley..

The Golden Fleece

John Winchcombe, alias Smalwoode, was more popularly known as 'Jack of Newbury', and was the most famous of the Berkshire clothiers who lived during the reigns of Henry VII and Henry VIII. He began as an apprentice of a rich clothier in Newbury when the trade was at its height, married his employer's widow and became prosperous in his own right. Deloney, in his book "The Pleasant History of John Winchcombe", described the scenes within the Tudor clothing establishment:

Within one room, being large and long,
There stood two hundred looms full strong.
Two hundred men, the truth is so,
Wrought in their loomes all in a row.
By every one a prettie boy
Sate making quills with mickle joy;
And in another place hard by
An hundred women merrily
Were carding hard with joyful cheere,
Who singing sat with voyces cleere.
And in a chamber close beside,
Two hundred maydens did abide.
In peticoats of stammel red,
And milk-white kerchers on their head;
Their smocke sleeves like to winter snow
That on the westerne mountaines flow,
And each sleeve with a silken band
Was featly tied at the hand;
These prettie maids did never lin
But in their place all day did spin;
And spinning so with voyces meet,
Like nightingales they sung full sweet.
Then to another loom came they,
Where children were in poor array.
And every one sat picking woll
The fineste from the course to pull.
The number was seven score and ten,
The children of poor silly men.
And these, their labours to requite,
Had every one a penny at night
Beside their meate and drink all day,
Which was to them a wondrous stay.
Within another place likewise
Full fiftie proper men he spies;
And these were shearemen every one,
Whole skills and cunning there was showne.
And hard by them there did remaine
Full foure score rowers taking paine.
A dye-house likewise had he then,
Wherein he kept full fortie men;
And likewise in his fulling mill,
Full twenty persons kept he still.

A 16th century cloth merchant's shop.

The fulling mill in question was at Bagnor, near Speen where a waste ground called Rock Marsh adjoined the mill, a series of posts outlined the framework for drying the cloth.

The Royal County of Berkshire

Deloney, describes the scene and tells of "warehouses, some being filled with wool, some with flocks, some with woad and madder, and some with broadcloth and kersies ready dyed and drest, beside a great number of others, some stretched on the tenters, some hanging on poles, and a great many more lying wet in other places". This may be taken as an accurate description of the Newbury clothing establishment. John Winchcombe took a leading part among the English clothiers in trying to obtain freedom of trade with foreign countries at a time when war prevented any sales to France and the Low Countries. He was offered a Knighthood but declined it preferring "to rest in his russet-coat a poor clothier to his dying day".

Another Newbury clothier of note was Thomas Dolman who had a factory in Northbrook Street. He was more ambitious than Winchcombe, and after attaining great wealth, built Shaw House at a cost of £10,000.

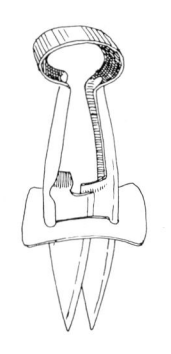

The manufacturers of the Tudor period were very prosperous. The Inclosure Acts of 1517–8 show that a very large amount of arable land in Berkshire was laid down as sheep pasture, in order to produce rich fleeces for the trade. The industry was firmly established in Reading by this date, the earliest mention being in 1435 when Nicholas Mountfort, a fuller, and John Heryng, a weaver, were admitted as members of the Guild. In a charter of 1485 the King gave authority to the mayor and burgesses for "the working and making of cloth, and examining the utensils employed in the same."

Sheep shears.

After the Inclosure Acts the supply of wool to the Reading clothiers became more plentiful, as did the labour force from those who flocked to the towns for employment. Merchants and manufacturers became rich and prosperous and the Clothiers and Clothmakers Company was prominent among the gilds. Queen Elizabeth I encouraged the trade, which was at its peak during her reign. She built some cottages in the abbey precincts for some imported Flemings.

A 17th century weaver.

Amongst the most famous of the Reading clothiers was John Kendrick, who is said to have kept 140 looms in constant use, whereby several hundred labourers, pickers, sorters, carders, spinners, weavers, dyers and teazers were kept in employment. He was a generous benefactor and when he died in 1624 part of his large fortune went towards building a large house where the poor could be constantly employed. He also left amounts of money which would help to subsidise poor clothiers in the town, but unfortunately this donation had the reverse effect as the money was misappropriated and given to selected traders who were able to undercut the prices of the smaller clothiers eventually driving them out of business. Eventually the Civil War killed the industry in the town.

At Wallingford the clothing trade was carried on from early times. Cloth was being sold in the market in 1233, and clothiers appear as a list of traders in 1227 together with weavers and fullers. Woolcarters are mentioned in 1265 and a fulling mill in the year 1540.

The cloth trade was not confined to the town and in many villages each cottage had its own spinning wheel. Every week the clothiers in the towns sent out men with packhorses laden with wool, and returned with packs laden with yarn ready for the loom. East Hendred is a good example of a prosperous village where this activity took place and where a fulling mill existed in 1547 held from the King by John Tyson.

At Newbury manufacture continued well into the nineteenth century where in 1808 kerseys, cottons, calicoes, linen and damask were still being made. In 1811 Sir John Throckmarton had such faith in one clothier that he wagered him one thousand guineas that he could not make a coat between sunrise and sunset from wool taken that morning from the sheep's back. The clothier was John Coxeter of Greenham Mills, who actually accomplished the task and presented the coat to the baronet the same evening. The garment was exhibited at the Great Exhibition of 1851.

The industry in Berkshire finally fizzled out when the large manufacturing districts in Lancashire and Yorkshire took over. One of the last towns to make cloth was Abingdon, which curiously enough may well have been the first, manufacturing under the auspices of the Great Abbey.

The Golden Fleece

Spinning wool in the medieval period.

Brewing Dye for cloth in medieval times.

*The Royal County
of Berkshire*

A cloth hall at Newbury.

CHAPTER 10
Crime and Punishment

In the early medieval period when the manorial system was in being it was normal for criminals, or offenders, to be tried locally in courts set up within their own manor. In Berkshire most large manors had their own pair of gallows, whipping posts or similar torture devices with which to inflict a suitable punishment as determined by the court. The whole point of the feudal system was to treat the manor and its inhabitants as an isolated unit, self-sufficient in most things, so it was not surprising that local justice was to be preferred. The results of these cases are to be found in the court rolls of the specific manors, which are an invaluable source of information.

The abbots of the large religious houses as at Abingdon, Reading and Hurley also had judicious powers. From the reign of Henry II the assizes for the settlement of land cases were actively employed in Berkshire and disputes over rights of pasture were an endless source of litigation. In communal cases the practice was for the neighbouring hundreds to present their pleas of the crown before justices at some central place and the decision as to whether or not they were guilty was made by jurors.

Murders were frequent and often committed by wandering strangers rather than the inhabitants within a manor, and were punishable by hanging or outlawry. Flight from justice also led to outlawry, whether or not the fugitives were guilty. Murderers on the run were liable to be killed by anyone.

The Royal County of Berkshire

Theft was the commonest of crimes and was punished as severely as taking a life. If the thief was caught red-handed he was almost certain to be hanged. William of Cookham, who had been captured with four stolen hens, however, was only imprisoned at Reading, although later the whole hundred sentenced him to lose an ear. Prisons of medieval times were not often used for long imprisonments, but more often for temporary detention. It would seem that most prisons were easy to escape from, and there are many records of a village being fined because one of their inhabitants escaped whilst on remand. Another important reason was the cost of keeping someone in gaol, so it was more profitable to let him off with a heavy fine which he paid to the exchequer.

The village itself was often fined if a corpse was found within its boundaries, so it was fairly common to find cases where the corpse was hurriedly buried or thrown into a river to avoid the fine. This could result in an increased fine. Two other crimes had been added to the pleas of the crown by the reign of Henry III. These were offences concerning coinage and arson, which was punished by outlawry and forfeiture of the felon's goods.

As courts of itinerant justices became more active the manorial courts resorted more to the investigation of rural crimes and the making of by-laws. Rural offenses included allowing animals to trespass on the land of others, putting too many beasts out to graze on common land or allowing the wrong sort of animal to graze. Neglecting to do work for the lord of the manor or performing badly whilst carrying it out were also offences. Such offences also applied to the clergy as in the case of the Vicar of Bourton who was fined for letting his sheep go on forbidden ground and the chaplain of Brightwalton who was convicted of breaking down the lord's hedges and stealing his fowls.

A few crimes of violence were tried in the manorial courts, but these were mainly quarrels between estate workers. The more serious cases of violence usually occurred in the towns. One man at Wallingford had his house broken into, his horse carried off, and his wife injured, and the damage was estimated at 3 shillings and fourpence for the horse but only two shillings for the wife! Agnes Pain was fined five shillings for beating a maidservant so severely that she had to lie in bed for fifteen days.

Combe Gibbet.

Crime and Punishment

As early as 1233 slander was considered a punishable offence. At Brightwalton a tenant dropped a case of verbal injury by a woman on payment of one shilling. Cursing was another offence, and women were the chief offenders being branded "scandal-mongers" and common scolds. In most cases fines were the normal solution or perhaps the tumbrel or cucking stool as in Wallingford.

The judicial system was not without its weak points and corruption. When Edward I inspected the system he found that sheriffs were freeing prisoners in return for money and jurors receiving presents from the accused in return for swearing in his favour. One coroner in Abingdon refused to examine a body until he was given a bribe of 1,000 herrings even though his son had already stolen the dead man's tunic. At Windsor in 1314 the burgesses petitioned that their gaol might be removed because they were too poor to keep it properly, so that the accused often died before justice was done. Even at Reading Gaol in the opening years of Richard II's reign, men were found dead for lack of food, because no one knew who ought to make provision for the prisoners.

By the seventeenth century the manorial courts were meeting less regularly and were being superseded. The courts of Cookham and Bray who had formerly met every three weeks, now only met four times a year at the most, whilst the forest court at Windsor still met regularly to consider cases of poaching. Fines were often levied by church wardens for offences such as swearing, drunkenness, absence from church, drinking on Sunday or gambling. There was an increase in methods of punishment as in Hungerford where the cage, stocks, pillory and cucking stool were used. There were also whipping posts in most towns, used mainly for boys. In Reading there was a house of correction mainly for this purpose. In the higher courts harsher sentences were now being employed and in 1631 a boy was hanged for arson in Windsor.

By the eighteenth and nineteenth centuries the most important felonies were tried by the justices of the peace in their quarter sessions, although sentence of death was only inflicted at the assizes. In 1761 Ann Giles of Speenhamland was hanged for setting fire to a barn, and until quite late burglars could receive capital punishment. The most severe punishment that could be inflicted by the J.P.'s was transportation to one of the colonies,

Stocks.

The Royal County of Berkshire

and this was often given for petty larceny. At Reading Quarter Session this punishment was inflicted on Moses Mason for stealing a pair of stockings and other small items in 1771, and to others in 1774 for the theft of a male ass, and four cheeses. In 1830 several machine rioters suffered transportation at Newbury.

Imprisonment was often rendered more severe by the addition of hard labour or confinement in a solitary cell. In 1800 a man convicted of stealing goods worth 10 pence was sentenced to six months hard labour; every other fortnight in solitude. At Hungerford in 1822 a misdemeanour of "fraudulently obtaining two umbrellas" was punishable by three months hard labour.

In 1822 Reading Gaol set up a treadmill for the use of prisoners serving hard labour and Abingdon followed in 1827 but could only afford a handmill. In 1841 the chaplain at Reading did a survey and reported that out of 443 prisoners only 127 could read and write, 159 could do neither, and 157 could only read. He felt that illiteracy may well be a reason for their criminal activity. He also stated that there was a great increase in juvenile offenders, perhaps because they had to share cells with felons.

As with all counties, the administration of justice has improved in Berkshire and some of the more barbaric punishments have been discontinued. However, I suspect that the number of criminals has increased as we move into the last decade of the twentieth century.

CHAPTER 11
The Civil War (1642–51)

During the Civil War Berkshire suffered more than many other counties. Sandwiched between the Royalist forces in Oxford and the Roundheads in London the county was the scene of many conflicts which disrupted normal life and caused much destruction in the towns. The people had to endure the constant movement of troops across their land, the confiscation of their animals and cereals and the payment of heavy taxes to support the armies.

These demands came from both sides, depending on which army held a particular town or village at any one time. In Newbury, for instance, food and supplies assembled to help the Parliamentary cause were taken by the Royalist troops when they reached the town first. In country areas soldiers preyed on the farmers and took cattle, horses, sheep and corn by force. At Wargrave the timely arrival of some troopers prevented Royalists from taking five cartloads of wheat and 150 sheep from the village. At Wokingham soldiers from the Reading garrison ordered the townspeople to fill eight carts with firewood and bedding. When they failed to carry out the order four houses were destroyed and their occupants banished to Windsor. The village of Twyford, being at the centre of operations, had property pillaged almost every day and complained to Parliament in vain.

Major disruption was caused by the destruction of bridges, ferries and mills on the Thames, Loddon and Kennet rivers. This affected trade and communications, and at a later date both armies had cause to regret these rash acts. Armies on the move commandeered property for use in billeting soldiers who could never be certain whether they were with

A Cromwellian soldier.

The Royal County of Berkshire

friends or enemies. Loyalties were divided in settlements and even within families. Amongst the gentry brother fought against brother, as in the case of the Vachell and Blagrave families in Reading. Even the members of Reading Council had conflicting loyalties.

The Civil War began on 22nd August, 1642 when Charles I raised his standard at Nottingham against Parliament. The King was very at home in Windsor and intended the castle to be his HQ throughout the War. However, he felt that the town was too close to London for comfort and selected Oxford as his centre. The first battle of the War was at Edgehill on 23rd October, 1642, and five days later Windsor was occupied by the Parliamentary forces. It is perhaps ironic that this town, usually associated with royalty, was held as a Puritan garrison for the duration of the War.

Between 1642 and 1648 Windsor Castle acted as a prison for Royalist soldiers, whilst the Great Park was a training ground for the Parliamentary army. The permanent garrison at Windsor was set at 1,000 men, effectively doubling the population. However, in April 1643 the Earl of Essex arrived with some 16,000 foot and 3,000 mounted soldiers for whom the town was expected to cater. Many men were billeted with the townsfolk and paid for their lodgings, but usually in arrears. Large numbers had to camp out in the Great Park and by 1648 they had killed and eaten several thousand deer.

The CURFEW TOWER at Windsor Castle, used as a prison.

In April 1645 the New Model Army was formed at Windsor by Sir Thomas Fairfax. These were an élite trained company of professional soldiers brought together on the express orders of Cromwell. The House of Commons despatched large quantities of weapons to Windsor for their use and on 30th April 1645 the Army left Windsor for Taunton and their very threat caused the Royalists to abandon the town. Windsor remained a military centre to which disbanded soldiers returned for payment and work detail.

Whilst east Berkshire was ostensively in Parliamentary hands, the majority of the north and west of the county was under the control of the King. Two regiments of horse were stationed at Abingdon to defend the bridge across the Thames, which afforded passage from Oxford into Berkshire. At Wallingford the ancient castle, which had fallen into disuse, was re-fortified and several heavy canon positioned on the ramparts of the town. Warrants were issued demanding all arms to be brought to the castle.

At Reading a garrison of Roundheads had been set up by Henry Marten MP who had raised his own regiment of horse. The town, however, was unfortified and when on 1st November 1642 a party of mounted Royalists approached Reading, Marten abandoned the town. By 4th November the town was completely occupied by the Royalists and many of the leading townsmen welcomed the King. Charles remained there for four days and then advanced on London, but was obliged to withdraw and returned to Reading on 19th November.

Reading remained a Royalist stronghold until April 1643, and was the largest garrison town outside Oxford with over 3,000 soldiers quartered there. When the King returned to Oxford he placed a large burden on the town, expecting them to provide £500 for his campaign and pay taxes to cover all other essential supplies.

During the governship of Sir Arthur Aston, Reading was fortified with lines of ditches and ramparts which enclosed the town except in the areas where the Thames and Kennet provided natural defences. An earthern redoubt was built at the top of Castle Hill, in the Forbury and at other strategic points.

These defences were tested in the Seige of Reading which took place from the 15th to the 25th April, 1643. The Parliamentary forces under the Earl of Essex, after taking the town of

The Civil War (1642–51)

A Pikeman of the New Model Army.

King Charles I (Wenceslaus Hollar 1644).

The Royal County of Berkshire

Henley, assembled an army of 15,000 foot soldiers and 3,000 horsemen on Caversham heights, overlooking Reading. On 15th April the governor of Reading, who had a mere 3,000 foot and 300 horse was asked to surrender, but refused.

On 16th April Essex directed an attack on the Royalist defences by Caversham Bridge, destroying half of St Peters Church in a vicious onslaught. By evening he had taken the bridge and encamped his army in fields surrounding the town. Essex gained ground to the west of the town and set up his HQ at Southcote Manor. Whilst Essex was making headway from the west and north, the Royalists received reinforcements on 18th April in the form of 600 musketeers and ammunition which travelled up the Thames from Sonning. Notwithstanding this boost Colonel Fielding realised that the Royalist position was hopeless and hung out the white flag.

Whilst Fielding was discussing the terms of surrender with the Parliamentary forces the King and Prince Rupert arrived on Caversham Heights and made a further attack on the forces guarding the bridge, but marksmen picked off the Royalists as they swept down the hillside. They were forced to retreat leaving their dead on the battlefield and on 27th April the Royalist garrison marched out of Reading having been granted free passage to Oxford.

Reading remained in Parliamentary hands until September 1643 after which Essex withdrew his army to London. The town was re-occupied by Royalists and Charles visited Reading again in May 1644 when he was entertained at Coley Park. At that time the King decided to make no attempt to hold the town and by the 20th of the month Essex was once more in control. Parliamentary forces held the town until the end of the war.

The most decisive Civil War events that took place in Berkshire were the two battles which took place at Newbury in 1643 and 1644. Just prior to the first battle the Earl of Essex had relieved Gloucester with the Parliamentary troops and planned to return to London via Berkshire. Prince Rupert and the Royalists intercepted Essex within the county and a skirmish took place at Aldbourne Chase. That night Essex stayed with John Packer at Chilton whilst his troops bedded down in Hungerford. Several of the wounded died that night and were buried in the town.

Prince Rupert, the 'mad cavalier'.

The Civil War (1642–51)

The next day they re-assembled and marched on through Kintbury and Hamstead Marshall, arriving at Enborne on 19th September 1643. Essex had intended to bed down in Newbury that night but found that the town had been taken by the Royalists, who were drawn up on Wash Common. The Roundheads were very short of supplies and the men tired, hungry and wet. On top of this the Royalists outnumbered them by 2,000 men. That night they camped at Crockham Heath.

At dawn on 20th September Essex deployed his army and placed his right wing in front of Biggs Hill facing Prince Rupert and his cavalry, and his left wing at Enborne and Hamstead Park facing the King's Lifeguards. The main body which included the artillery were sited on a plateau to the west of Wheatlands Farm as a protection against the Royalists at Wash Common. The first Battle of Newbury was about to begin.

Fighting went on all the day and well into the night until both sides had to rest. The Roundheads were desperate for supplies and Essex prepared for another dawn attack. Unknown to them the Royalists had sustained heavy losses and were low on gunpowder and consequently the next morning Essex found that the Royalists had deserted Newbury during the night leaving the road to London open. Essex marched via Greenham Common and Brimpton and only encountered one small skirmish near Aldermaston.

Altogether 6,000 men fell in the battle and whilst many were buried on the battlefield, 60 cart loads of bodies were taken into Newbury. Four large mounds in the town are thought to contain the remains of these dead soldiers. Amongst those who fell were the Earls of Caernavon and Sunderland and Lord Falkland. A memorial to the latter was raised in 1878 on the corner of Essex Street and the Andover Road.

The 2nd Battle of Newbury took place on 27th October 1644 nearer Speen and around Donnington Castle and Shaw House, both of which were held for the Royalists by Colonel Boys. The Parliamentarians under the Earl of Manchester left Reading hoping to surprise the Royalists but found them ready and waiting. After considerable battle and loss of life, the King ordered his main army to return to Oxford whilst he returned to Bath, leaving most of his artillery at Donnington Castle.

The Earl of Essex at the first battle of Newbury.

The Royal County of Berkshire

The Castle was being defended by Sir John Boys and was continually under siege. In August 1644 it was attacked by General Middleton who lost 100 men and gained nothing. On 19th September a strong assault was made by Colonel Horton who managed to destroy three towers on the curtain wall. On each occasion Boys was asked to surrender but refused to do so. A further attempt was made on 7th November when Manchester returned with his entire army and encircled the fortification. After two days the King and Prince Rupert returned to Newbury and relieved the castle with 10,000 men. The castle was subject to many more sieges during the war but Colonel Boys held out until ordered by the King to surrender. The garrison moved out in April 1646.

At the east of the county Maidenhead came under the Parliamentarians. Maidenhead Thicket, to the west of town, was used as a training ground for the troops and on 19th October 1644 it was reported that the Earl of Manchester had 3,000 men encamped there. Maidenhead's historical event did not occur until nearer the end of the war when Charles I had been caught and imprisoned with Lord Craven at Caversham.

Knowing that he was going to die he made a request to see his three children for the last time. Sir Thomas Fairfax put his request before Parliament and it was agreed that this would be a human act. Accordingly, Charles was escorted from Caversham to Maidenhead where his children awaited him. His route was strewed with green boughs and flowers from well wishers. When he reached Maidenhead he held the baby Duke of Gloucester in his arms and comforted the Princess Elizabeth and the young Duke of York. Cromwell, a hardened man, confessed that he had never been present at so tender a scene. Refreshments were taken at the

DONNINGTON CASTLE.

Greyhound Inn in the High Street, after which the whole family was driven back to Caversham and said their last farewells after two days. The date of their final meeting had been 16th July 1647.

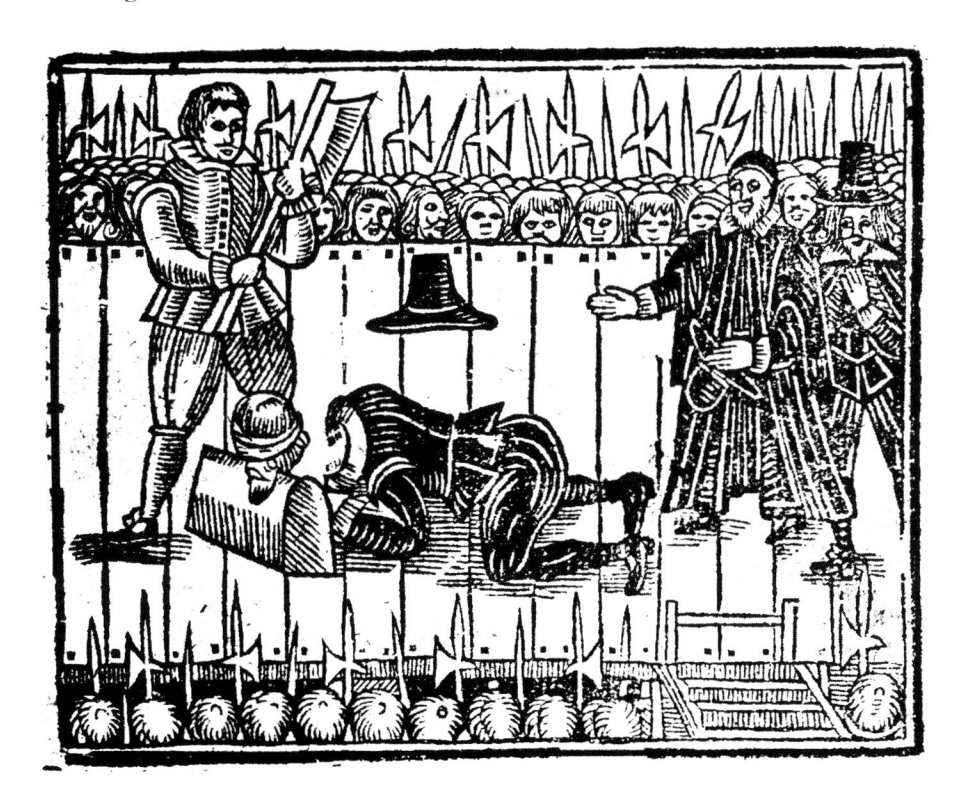

King Charles was transferred to Windsor Castle along with his two dogs. On 19th January 1649 he was taken to London for his trial which took place in Westminster Hall. He was sentenced to death and executed at Whitehall ten days later. His coffin was brought back to Windsor Castle and on 9th February he was buried with some ceremony in St George's Chapel. The King had returned to his favourite town.

The Civil War (1642–51)

Sir Thomas Fairfax of Caversham.

The execution of Charles I.

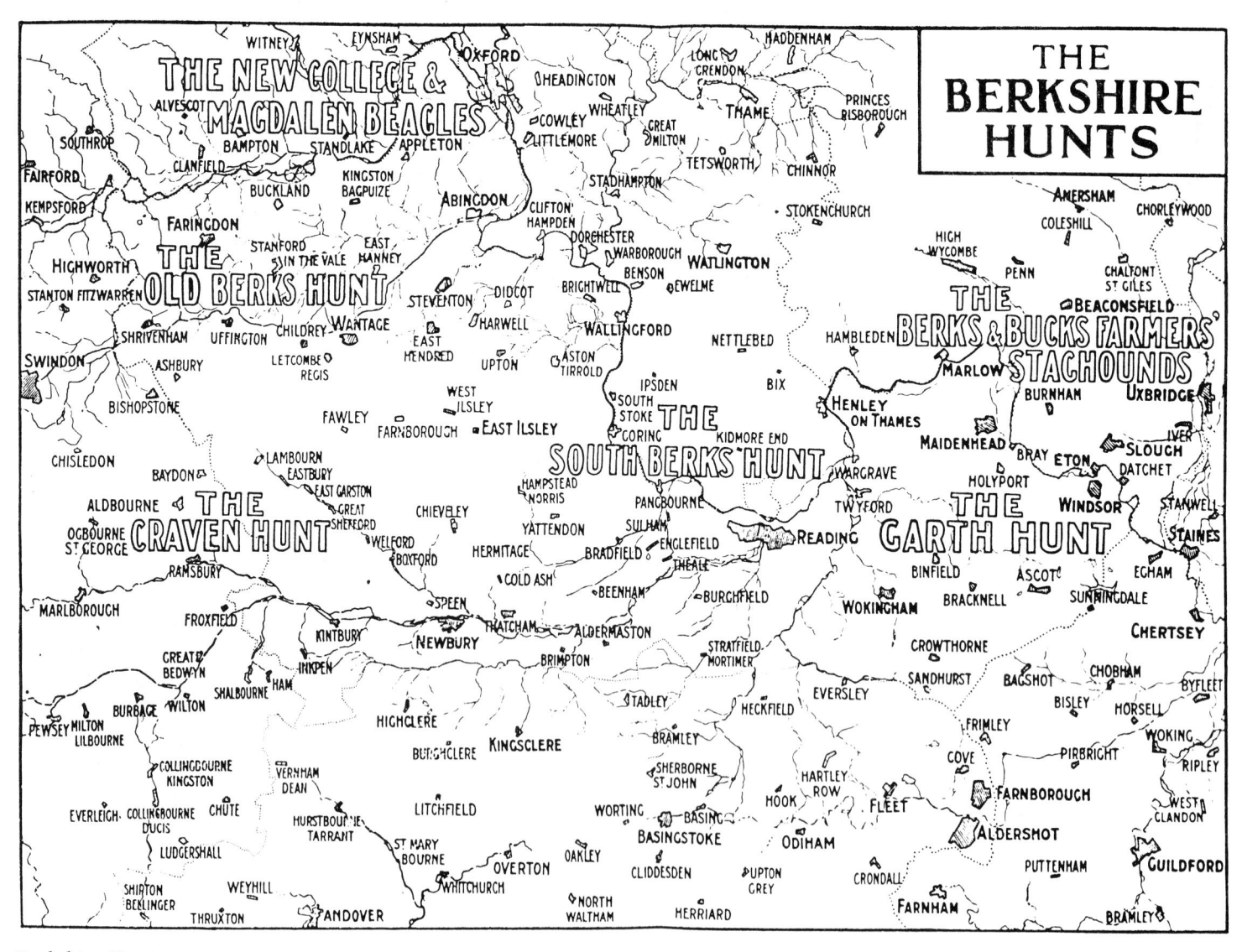

Berkshire Hunts.

CHAPTER 12
Ancient Sports and Pastimes

Hunting, as we have seen, is one of the oldest sports in the county as we know this was the practice of the Saxon Kings and in particular Edward the Confessor in his forest at Windsor. Perhaps the best known and earliest of the organised hunts was the Royal Buckhounds, of which Osborne Lavel, chamberlain to Henry II, was the first master. Later the position was held by the Brocas family who held lands in Clewer, Windsor, Eton, Cookham and Bray. The royal pack consists of twenty-four running dogs and six greyhounds.

Henry VIII, once again in fickle mood, decided to inaugurate his own private pack of buckhounds and these were the forerunners of the pack known as the Royal Buckhounds. Queen Mary did away with the sport but it was revived by Queen Elizabeth and was flourishing during the reign of James I. The first master of the privy pack was George, brother to Anne Boleyn, who shared his sister's fate, changing to the Earl of Leicester who was the Queen's favourite in Elizabethan times.

Queen Anne, devoted to hunting, amalgamated the two royal packs and built the kennels on the site of those in use until the pack was abolished in 1901. She increased the number of deer in the Royal Forest and in 1712 one hundred red deer were bought to stock up at Windsor. She herself hunted on horseback and made several rides in the forest for her own convenience. George III was another keen huntsman and in 1780 chased one stag for thirty miles from Windsor to Compton.

A lady riding with the Royal Buckhounds.

The Royal County of Berkshire

There were other staghounds including those of the eccentric Lord Barrymore of Wargrave who bought a pack of hounds in 1788 and kept them at Twyford with four liveried negroes. He had to purchase his own deer, four in all, two of which were old and blind and a third which was so tame it sidled up to the hounds. His set up came to an end in 1793 when he was shot in his twenty-fourth year.

Fox hunting is not a particularly ancient sport and mainly originated in the eighteenth century. One of the earliest recorded was the Craven Hunt which hunted in western Berkshire in 1739. The dogs were kennelled at Walcot and Kintbury. Another early promoter of the sport was John Elwes, reported to be a miser from Marcham who later became an MP for Berkshire. Mr William Chute, who originated the Vine in 1790, hunted in the south of the county, next to an area hunted by Stephen Poyntz of Midgham House. His huntsman was seldom sober and often lost most of the hounds who had to find their own way home.

Sir John Cope had kennels at Bramshill and near the Bath Road at Reading but in 1843 gave his portion of country to Mr Mortimer Thoyts of Sulhamstead who originated the South Berks Hunt. The Garth Hunt operated on territory east of the river Loddon and the old Berkshire Hunt was taking place by 1766.

A Roe Deer.

At the beginning of the eighteenth century there were also numerous packs of harriers in Berkshire. A picture of 1709 depicts hare-hunting at Park Place, Remenham. In the east of the county Prince Albert had his own pack, which later passed to Lord Desborough who hunted once a week. At the western end James Morrell had kennels at Bradley Farm near Cumnor by about 1840, for the pack known as the Berkshire Vale Harriers.

If we now consider fox hunting to be a cruel sport, then Bull Baiting and Cock Fighting were even more blood thirsty. Bull Baiting was considered to be a good form of entertainment by many of the rustics, who held contests on the village green. The bulls fought with bull dogs most prized by their owners, who put silver collars around their necks with tokens heralding past victories. The favourite day for the biggest event in this category was Good Friday. Bulls were by no means cheap animals and benefactors like

A Red Deer.

George Staverton put aside money from their estate to provide the animals, and as if to make up for the cruelty they stipulated that the meat from the dead bull should be given to the poor, and its hide for shoes.

Bracknell was famous for its 'bull fights' as was Wokingham, where the whole town turned out with the mayor and aldermen occupying seats in the Old Red Lion Inn. Regular fights also took place in the market place at Wallingford and at Wantage in the precincts of 'The Camel' inn. Wantage was said to be a town of rough characters who liked savage sports and tended to have encampments of pedlars, hawkers and gypsies on its outskirts. Bull baiting was prohibited after 1835.

Bull Baiting.

'Cocking' or Cock Fighting was another favourite sport in the county; and Shrove Tuesday was the usual day for this pastime. The heels of the birds were often armed with steel spurs to add to the severity of the fight. The *Complete Gamester* rather inaptly described it as a "sport or pastime so full of delight and pleasure that no game in that respect is to be preferred before it".

Royal Windsor featured the sport and the *London Gazette* reports an important match there in 1684. Even at Ascot Races the day's events usually ended with a match as in 1798 when it was announced that "during Ascot Races will be fought the great main of cocks at the Crown Inn, Egham, between the gentlemen of Surrey and Middlesex against the gentlemen of Kent and Sussex, for five guineas a battle and fifty the odd".

Wantage and Wokingham again featured in the tournaments and at the latter place the terraces surrounding the cockpit could be seen in the gardens

Cock Fighting.

Ancient Sports and Pastimes

The fourteenth century Bell Inn at Hurley.

of one of the houses. At the other end of the County an annual match took place in Whitsun Week at Market Ilsley between the gentlemen of Ilsley, Harwell, Wallingford and other towns in the Vale.

Badger Baiting was also practised in Wantage among the rough community and at Newbury a variation of throwing broomsticks at a cock tied to a stake was regarded as barbaric and suppressed in 1750.

When it comes to horse racing Berkshire can claim to be one of the most celebrated counties. At Lambourne, Wantage and other areas of the downs there are many important stables where champions of the turf have been trained, and at Ascot perhaps the best known course of all. Racing seems to have taken place from around the time of James I and certainly Charles II often frequented the course at Datchet Mead whilst staying in Windsor.

Often called the sport of Kings, the credit in Berkshire must be given to Queen Anne who started the Ascot Races. Before that she attended meetings at Datchet Mead where in 1709 it was reported that "Colonel Moreton won the Queen's Plate and the Earl of Bridgewater that of the town of Windsor". The first race at Ascot Heath took place in 1711, when Swift reported that "While at Windsor, Dr Arbuthnot, the Queen's physician and favourite, went out with me to show me the places; we overtook Miss Forester, a maid of honour, on her palfrey taking the air; we saw a place they have made for a famous horse race tomorrow when the Queen will come".

From the outset Ascot Races not only drew the patrons of the turf, but because of its royal associations, the *élite* of fashionable society. Fashions were bold, and the aforementioned Miss Forester, who was considered the reigning beauty of her day, turned up at the initial meeting dressed like a man, with a long white riding coat, full flapped waistcoat and a three cornered cocked hat.

Of the surviving race courses Windsor and Newbury are perhaps the best known, although the race course near Clewer which bears the name Windsor is relatively modern, replacing

Reading Races in King's Meadow, 1844

Ascot Races 1843: The Grand Stand

The Royal County of Berkshire

the most ancient course at Datchet Mead. At Newbury, however, races were held on the Wash as early as 1749. Of the discontinued courses Abingdon is one of the oldest commencing in 1733 on Culham Heath for the Galloway Plate donated by Abingdon Corporation. The last meeting was in 1875, and the grandstand was pulled down in 1890 by the Town Council. Reading Races began on 23rd July 1747, when a purse of 50 sovereign was won by a black horse belonging to Lord William Manners. The course seemed to attract a good selection of local gentry, who attended an annual ball. Mr Philip Powys recorded in his diary for 1788 that "the races not good, the balls tolerably full considering how many families at this season leave their seats in the country for the different watering places now in vogue", and in 1801 the *Reading Mercury* reported that "the races offered good sport, every heat being strongly attended. The balls were honoured with a most brilliant display of all the fashion and beauty in the neighbourhood". The site of Reading Races was at Bulmershe Heath and was moved to King's Mead in 1813. The races were discontinued in 1873.

Maidenhead Race course was located on Maidenhead Thicket and was in fashion during the eighteenth century. The whole of the Royal family visited on 27th September 1787, but the meetings were short lived. Racing is recorded at East Ilsley between 1764 and 1800 and a new course opened at Newbury in 1905. There were also steeplechasing courses at Hawthorn Hill, near Maidenhead and at Maiden Erleigh, near Reading.

Considering how long the Thames river has been in existence, one would have thought that boat races would have taken place from the earliest times. However, rowing seems to have predominately started during the Victorian period, during which most large towns on the river held their own regattas. The most famous of these is undoubtedly Henley, which although itself in Oxon, uses the Berkshire bank at Remenham to pitch the marquees. The first regatta was held here in 1839, but it first became royal in 1851 after accepting Prince Albert as its first Patron. Since his death the reigning sovereign has always consented to fill this position. Nowadays this is a special event in the Thames diary and was used in 1908 and 1948 to stage the Olympic rowing events.

The medieval barn at Great Coxwell.

The Royal County of Berkshire

In addition to the regattas the two public schools Radley and Eton were often matched against each other and the former provided rowers for the Oxford crew in the annual boat race.

In contrast to rowing, archery must have been perhaps the oldest sport practised in the county. By the nature of the sport, and the fact that bows and arrows were used at the time of the Norman Conquest, contests must have featured regularly in any medieval tournaments. Henry VIII was particularly fond of archery and was often annoyed with villages that did not provide facilities as at Cookham where it was reported that "the tithing man presents that there are no archery butts, and the inhabitants are ordered to provide them under penalty!" Many names linger on as in St Mary's Butts, Reading where tournaments took place. Archery meetings took place at Old Field at Bray, as recorded by a brass plate in Clewer Church which reads:

Medieval archers at the Butts.

> *He that lieth under this stone,*
> *Shott with a hundred men, himselfe alone;*
> *This is trew that I do say,*
> *The match was shott in Ould Felde at Bray,*
> *I will tell you before you go hence,*
> *That his name was Martine Expence.*

Whether this inscription records his victory against a hundred men or whether he died by the arrow is not too clear. However, except for this early tournament there is little recorded of archery clubs until 1831 when the West Berks Club seems to have held a distinguished place. The shoots took place at two lodges, one at Beenham Place, and the other at Sparsholt House, near Wantage.

A Wolfhound.

In comparison with the contests between man and beast, where the animals were always the loser, savage bouts between humans, although just as bloody, at least provided a chance for either side to win. Before the Marquess of Queensbury set the rules for boxing, the sport which came under the heading of pugilism was very popular. Fist fights without any ground rules seem to have been the order of the day and many contests within Berkshire are recorded. It would seem that as the county was close to London, it was a favourite battleground for contestants.

The earliest recorded bout seems to have been at Reading in 1759 when John Slack, the champion of the day, made mincemeat of an aspiring cowman named Moreton. Henry Sellers was champion for four years from 1777 to 1781, having defeated Joe Hood at Ascot Heath during the race week in 1777. Thousands flocked to Wokingham on 18th June 1787 to see a battle between another champion Tom Johnson with a west country man named Bill Warr. Apparently Warr adopted cowardly tactics and feigned injury but eventually ended up out cold.

Wargrave was a noted centre of pugilism under the patronage of the Earl of Barrymore. He engaged many of the stalwarts of the ring and paid for their lodging at the George Inn. The Earl thought it was amusing to match these worthies against his house guests who always came off the worst for wear. The *Reading Mercury* of 7th December 1789 records that: "On Monday a battle was fought between Hooper, the noted tinman, and Wright, the noted carpenter of Binfield Heath, which lasted about 25 minutes, when the carpenter was so much beaten, particularly about the head and face, as to be obliged to give the victory to the tinman!"

Most of these combats were considered illegal, and a blood thirsty contest between Tom Belcher and Joe Berks at Hurley Bottom ended in the arrest of everyone "for unlawfully assembling and publicly fighting". All were bailed out except Berks, the unfortunate loser, who was sent to Reading gaol.

If pugilism was considered to be the sophisticated side of personal combat then the rustics, particularly in White Horse Vale, adopted much cruder sports. One of these was Cudgel-Play, whereby the contestants had to inflict blows on each others head until one of them drew blood and was declared the victor. Such brain bashing was enough to produce a whole race of village idiots. Popular venues for this activity were Bulmershe Heath and

Ancient Sports and Pastimes

A Wild Boar.

A Prize Fighter.

The Royal County of Berkshire

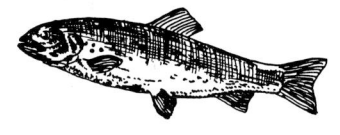

The Trout.

The Perch.

The Gudgeon.

the 'Chequers' at Woodley.

This sport was a great favourite amongst the activities that took place during the ceremony of the Scouring of the White Horse of Uffington which was recorded from 1755. Often up to 30 thousand people attended to enjoy the day out. In 1785 Harry Stanley, landlord of the 'Blowing Stone', proved the champion with the cudgel and Farmer Smallbones of Sparsholt beat all comers at wrestling.

A game peculiar to Berkshire was Kick-Shins, which often occurred outside a public house between two carters who had stopped for sustenance. The men kicked each others shins with hobnailed boots until one submitted and agreed to buy the drinks. A similar contest was Cut-Legs which was achieved by lashing each others legs with a carters whip.

Of the two most popular sports Cricket and Football, there are numerous records throughout the County and it is probably only relevant to mention the earliest matches. Bray, near Maidenhead, seems to have been the main centre of Berkshire cricket and the earliest mention of the game seems to be in 1793 when the Maidenhead Club played the MCC at Lord's Cricket Ground. Mr Lord himself played for the MCC, but the match ended in victory for Maidenhead. In the return match four weeks later Maidenhead won again.

We complain of football hooligans nowadays, but the first mention of the game in Berkshire seems to have been particularly violent. The church register at North Moreton, near Didcot records in 1598 Richard and John Gregorie were buried and that "these two men were killed by ould Gunter; Gunteres sonnes and the Gregories fell together by yeyeares. At Football Gunter drew his dagger and broke booth there heades and they died booth within a fortnight later".

It would appear that 'Ould Gunter' was the parson of the parish, and witnessed his sons losing the game. Carried away in the excitement he drew his dagger and stabbed the other two boys, who died. It is a curious story, as the parson does not seem to have been punished for his unsportsmanlike act. Strange to say this isolated game of football in the 16th century is the only early record until 1874 when a game was played in Slough.

Ancient Sports and Pastimes

Hunting scenes on medieval tiles.

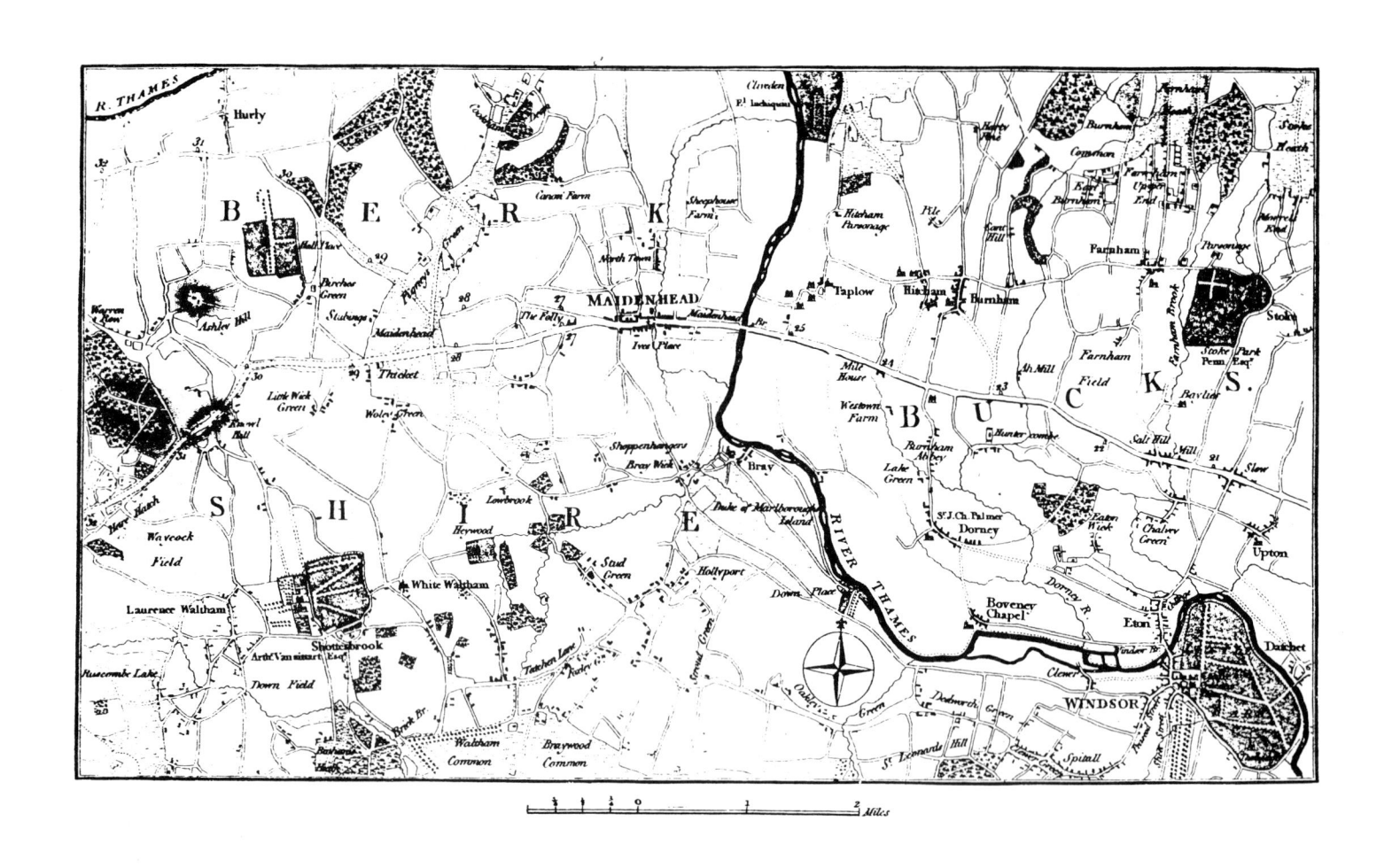

Windsor and East Berkshire (Robertson 1792).

CHAPTER 13
Communications, Coaching and Canals

Most major communications within the county whether on land or water tend to run from east to west or in the case of the river Thames from west to east. This being so all roads, rivers and canals have been used as intermediate parts of a route between London and the important port of Bristol. Even in Roman times the Devil's Highway passed through the south of the county via Staines and Silchester on its way to the temple of Sulis Minerva at Bath or the port facilities at Sea Mills near Avonmouth.

In the Anglo-Saxon period entry into Berkshire from the east was always hampered by a need for a crossing over the river Thames. From London traffic entered the county by a ford and ferry both at Datchet and Cookham. The former took passengers through Windsor, Clewer and Bray along the bounds of the Old Windsor Forest and then to Reading, whilst the latter led to the early county town of Wallingford. A north-south road, now represented by the A34, linked the important Saxon towns of Oxford and Southampton via Winchester.

By the 13th century there were wooden bridges across the Thames at both Maidenhead and Windsor which provided easier access into the county. However, roads were little more than tracks, with rough surfaces and potholes. It was perhaps due to Queen Anne that improvements were made to the highways at the beginning of the 18th century. It was in 1702 when the queen, who was a partial invalid and suffered from gout and dropsy, decided to take the waters at Bath and where she went society followed. The city became a popular resort and the highway from

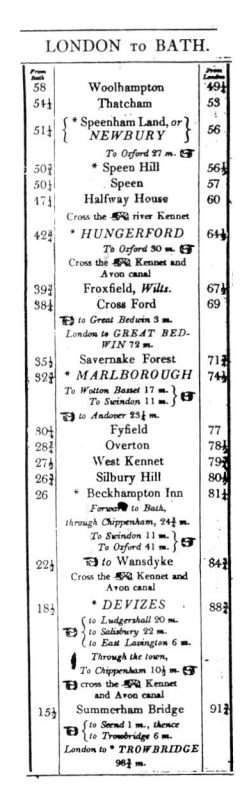

The Coaching route through Berkshire (1).

The Royal County of Berkshire

London became known as the Bath Road.

A survey was carried out in 1709 and some improvements made to the Bath Road but nevertheless passengers still travelled in some discomfort and regular stopping places became essential. When stage coaches were introduced they were heavy and required up to six horses, which had to be changed every ten miles at 'stages'. In many coaches only six passengers could be accommodated, which made the journey quite expensive so that only the middle classes could afford to use this public transport. The rich travelled in their own coaches or privately hired post-chaises. The coaches would enter the courtyard of an inn through an arched driveway or by a lane at the rear of the establishment. Whilst the passengers were taking refreshments ostlers and grooms rushed around changing or stabling the horses.

All towns and villages along the route of the Bath Road benefited from the increased traffic. In a survey carried out in 1834 at Maidenhead statistics showed that 823 coaches passed through the town involving the use of 3,000 horses. Maidenhead became a popular first stop on the route to Bristol and catered handsomely for the travellers providing inns and stabling, blacksmiths, farriers, coachmakers, saddlers and wheelwrights.

Maidenhead had at least six coaching inns. From the London direction the first of these was the Orkney Arms, later rebuilt as the famous Skindles Hotel. In the High Street were the Red Lion, the Bear Inn, the Saracen's Head and the White Hart, whilst at the bottom of Castle Hill was the Sun, perhaps the largest of all. There was stabling for between 30 and 40 horses. From here John Piggott had the responsibility of leading westbound coaches to the top of Castle Hill which he did by attaching an extra pair of horses. Horses used in this way were known as 'cock' horses as mentioned in the Banbury Cross nursery rhyme.

From Maidenhead coaches travelling to Gloucester left the county at Henley on Thames. Both these and those heading for Bristol always had to run the hazard of crossing the notorious Maidenhead Thicket. At this time it was said to be five miles in diameter and a

The Coaching route through Berkshire (2)

134

Communications, Coaching and Canals

refuge for footpads, robbers and highwaymen. Many passengers who had not been robbed of their belongings whilst crossing Hounslow Heath lost them when crossing the Thicket. In local tradition, there is a story that the Vicar of Hurley in the reign of Elizabeth I "was allowed an extra salary for the danger of passing the Thicket", but as he collected it in Maidenhead he probably lost it on the way home! Another story tells of a certain highwayman who was an ostler at the Sun Inn. After having robbed the travellers on a coach, he would then sympathise with them when they arrived at the Inn. One day he was found in the loft bleeding, having been mortally wounded by a passenger on the coach who was now vainly looking for his services as an ostler.

When travellers reached Reading they had the choice of the Crown in Crown Street or the Bear in Bridge Street. Other flourishing inns included the George, the Ship or the Sun and the Broad Face or Saracen's Head in the Market Place. On the Bath run Reading was more than often the lunch stop after which the Crown at Theale provided cakes and ale in the late afternoon.

A Highwayman.

The most notable overnight stop was at Speenhamland, which is now part of the borough of Newbury. Here there was a variety of coaching inns, of which the George and Pelican was the most famous. It was recorded as existing as early as 1646 and boasted many important visitors. It was reputed to be a costly establishment as suggested by the local nursery rhyme:

Palmer's Postal Coach 1784.

> *"The famous inn at Speenhamland,*
> *That stands below the hill,*
> *May well be called the Pelican*
> *From its enormous bill"*

Speenhamland was roughly half way between London and Bristol and was a busy place in the 18th century. Both day and night the sound of the guard's horn, the crack of the whip and the rattle of wheels could be heard in the hamlet. There was a record number of inns

A Post Chaise.

135

The Royal County of Berkshire

including the Chequers, the Angel, the Bacon Arms, the Cross Keys, the Lamb & Flag, the King's Arms and the Old Globe. The Bear at Speen had been there since the Civil War and received the bodies of Lords Caernavon and Falkland. It also sported a cockpit.

The White Hart was the inn where the first 'Flying Coach' started in 1752. This had been developed in Newbury by John Clark and Coy and travelled from Newbury to London in 12 hours at the rate of five miles per hour. It carried four passengers who each paid ten shillings return fare. By 1784 the Palmers mail coach had been introduced and the journey from London to Bath took only two days but was still an uncomfortable experience.

At Speenhamland a popular theatre was built in 1802 to entertain the travellers who were staying overnight. Eight miles further on the important market town of Hungerford also prospered with the Bath Road where coaching inns were situated in Charnham Street and High Street. The most notable were the Three Swans, the Red Lion, the Stag's Head, the Lamb, the Sun, the Craven Arms and the Bear which could be traced back to 1494. The next section of the road through Savernake Forest was mentioned in a document of 1228 as 'the King's Street, leading from the house of the lepers at Hungerford towards Marlborough', and corresponds with the route of the modern A4 through the forest. A bridge was built over the Kennet at Hungerford in 1275 for the benefit of travellers on this road. This section of the Bath Road was improved in an Act of 1744 repairing the turnpike from Newbury to Marlborough.

Five different companies operated the Bath Road through Hungerford each offering greater comfort, punctuality and speed. Before the Royal Mail coaches each vehicle bore its own name amongst which was The Emerald, The Age, The Monarch and The

A Stage Wagon.

Regulator. But in the end all stage coaches became redundant very suddenly with the coming of the railway in 1843.

The river Thames forms the northern boundary of the county from Windsor to Oxford and as such has always been an important means of communication since prehistoric times. Many of the historic Berkshire towns like Windsor, Maidenhead, Reading, Wallingford and Abingdon were sited on the river from the outset illustrating its importance as a working waterway. Wharves set up on the river allowed heavy goods to be transported anywhere between Oxford and London. Oaks and timber from Windsor Forest were despatched from Windsor and Maidenhead for the repair of bridges and timber framed buildings, whilst stone was carried along the Thames for the building of Windsor Castle and Reading Abbey. By the 18th century navigation on the river was organised, and horse drawn barges carried most bulky goods such as coal, wood, salt or malt.

It is not within the scope of this book to relate a history of the Thames navigation and it is probably sufficient to say that in the 18th century 95% of goods despatched were carried by water. In 1722 Daniel Defoe described the county town of Reading as follows:

"It is a very large and wealthy town, handsomely built, the inhabitants rich and driving a very great trade. The town lies on the river Kennet, but so near the Thames, that the largest barges which they use may come up to the town bridge, and there they have wharfs to load, and unload them. Their chief trade is by this water navigation to and from London, though they have necessarily a great trade into the country, for the consumption of the goods which they bring by their barges from London, and particularly coals, salt, grocery wares, tobacco, oyls, and all heavy goods. They send from hence to London by these barges very great quantities of malt and meal, and these are the two principal articles of their loadings of which, so large are those barges, that some of them as I was told, bring a thousand or twelve hundred quarters of malt at a time, which according to the ordinary computation of tonnage in the freight of other vessels, is from a hundred, to a hundred and twenty ton, dead weight. They also send very large quantities of timber from Reading for Berkshire being a very well wooded county, and the river Thames a convenient conveyance for the timber. They send most of it, and especially the largest and fairest of the

Communications, Coaching and Canals

Swan upping on the Thames.

A Barge under way.

The riverside at Abingdon.

The Kennet at Newbury.

The Royal County of Berkshire

timber, to London, which is generally bought by shipwrights to the river, for the building of merchant ships; as also, the like trade of timber is at Henley, another town on the Thames and at Maidenhead".

The River Kennet at Sulhamstead.

The river Kennet which flowed through the town of Reading also served Newbury in the 17th century. Journeys from Reading, however, were slow and cumbersome with natural hazards such as shallows, rapids and floods and the need to create a head of water to drive mills. Waterborne trade had increased so much by 1700 that improvements to river navigation on the Kennet were essential.

In 1708 a scheme was put forward to improve the navigation between Newbury and Reading; but was strongly opposed by the traders in Reading who were afraid of losing their supremacy as the leading distribution centre for the county. Despite their opposition in delaying the project the Kennet Navigation Act was passed in 1714 and work commenced. In 1718 a new engineer, John Hore of Newbury, was appointed and he produced a plan to straighten out the meanders and reduce the course between Newbury and Reading to 18½ miles. A rise of 134 feet was to be overcome by the construction of 20 locks. This plan was approved and reached Burghfield by 1720.

In this year a mob from Reading, some 300 strong, which included the Recorder and the Mayor, Robert Blake, who owned a wharf in Reading, marched to the site and destroyed some of the canal workings, while others broke down new locks and sunk barges. The canal proprietors threatened prosecution after which the Mayor and Recorder undertook to keep the peace. Even so the bargemen passing through Reading suffered the ordeal of being stoned and threatened with violence. In July 1725 Bargemaster Peter Darvill of Maidenhead was warned that he would be shot and his vessel sunk if he passed through Reading again.

At Sheffield Mill, Theale, the miller diverted water through his mill gate effectively preventing the passage of barges through his lock. But as time passed it became obvious that the new waterway was in no way detrimental to the commercial interests of Reading and the harassment ceased. In time Newbury was able to build up a trade and both towns prospered.

Communications, Coaching and Canals

The Kennet and Avon Canal, a scheme to link London to Bristol via the Thames, Kennet and Avon rivers was first discussed in 1770 and brought to fruition by an Act in 1794. The building of this canal was avidly approved by those in Hungerford and the west of the county who could see the advantages. Work started at the Newbury end in October 1794 after the appointment of the engineer John Rennies. The first section between Newbury and Kintbury, a distance of six miles, was opened on 12th July 1797. The Kintbury to Hungerford section was opened in October 1798 and the Bath Chronicle reported that on "Tuesday, the ninth instant, a barge having on board a staircase of wrought Portland Stone for J Pearce esq of Chilton Lodge, and several casks of Russian tallow, making in the whole about 40 tons weight, was navigated on the Kennet & Avon Canal from Newbury to Hungerford".

The Kennet and the Great Western Railway.

The canal was finally opened in its entirety in December 1810 and brought more trade into Berkshire. By 1818 over 200 boats were using the canal, and some 70 were over 60 tons capacity. The wharf at Hungerford was especially busy loading gravel, chalk and whiting for the westerly route and timber for the east. Meanwhile the connection with Bristol brought new products from abroad, which included tea, iron, copper and pitch.

The Royal County of Berkshire

However, the use of the canal as a working waterway was short lived. With the coming of the railway, the barges, like the coaches, became redundant and the canal, which had cost £1 million to build sold to the Great Western Railway for £210,000.

The Lady Well at Speen.

Boulters Lock, Maidenhead between the wars.

CHAPTER 14
Victorian Expansion and the Railway

The idea of building the Great Western Railway from London to Bristol crossing the full width of Berkshire began in 1833 when merchants from Bristol showed dissatisfaction with the existing means of transporting goods to London. The route was painfully slow and goods were often delayed because of bad weather. Merchandise from Bristol was routed via the river Avon to Bath, then along the Kennet and Avon Canal to Reading and finally by Thames to London. The success of the Liverpool and Manchester Railway, which had opened in 1830 spurred the merchants into taking action.

In 1833 Isambard Kingdom Brunel, the engineer who had designed the Clifton Suspension Bridge, was appointed engineer for the GWR and made a preliminary survey of the route. On 30th July 1833 he put forward his proposals at a public meeting in Bristol where it was decided that a company be formed and that application should be made to Parliament. Two years of controversy followed whereby some were for and others against the project. As one might have expected, the Thames Navigation and other similar bodies opposed the scheme, and similarly several land owners along the route. However, by February 1835, the required capital had been raised and on 31st August of that year the Great Western Railway Bill was passed in the House of Lords.

Brunel began immediately to construct the first section of the line from Paddington to Maidenhead, which had been chosen as a temporary terminus, until such time as a bridge could be built across the Thames. He engaged a young 20 year old man, Daniel Gooch, to assist him with aspects of the building and choice of locomotives. Gooch was later to be

ISAMBARD KINGDOM BRUNEL.

The Royal County of Berkshire

Maidenhead Riverside Station.

Knighted and made Chairman of GWR. His family lived in Clewer, near Windsor, and his grave can be found in the churchyard there. His first tasks were to build the engine sheds at Paddington and Maidenhead and supervise the unloading of locomotives. Gooch had little faith in the early locomotives with the exception of the 'North Star', which was unloaded at Maidenhead Bridge from the barge which brought it from Newcastle. Whilst unloading the metal ropes snapped, killing one man and narrowly missing Brunel.

On 31st May 1838, the first GWR train left Paddington for Maidenhead, carrying the Directors of the line and their families, and the journey was completed in 49 minutes. On the 4th June the line was officially opened to the public and on the first day 1479 people travelled paying £226 for the privilege. It was not a comfortable journey but seemed to be quick despite the odd de-railments which occasionally occurred.

Two major engineering feats were required before the first section of the line in Berkshire could be completed between Maidenhead and Reading. The first of these was the bridge spanning the Thames at Maidenhead which had been designed by Brunel to be built in brick. The design contained two arches 128 feet wide which Brunel's critics said would fall down when the first train went over them. These were, and still are, the widest brick arches in the world. There was some minor distortion at first, which delighted the critics, but this was found to be the fault of the contractor. After this error had been corrected, Brunel ordered that the wooden centerings supporting the arches should be left in position for another winter. When in January 1840 a freak storm blew the centerings down, the bridge stood firm and its critics were silenced for ever.

On 1st July 1839 the line opened as far as Twyford, but before the railway could continue to Reading a second engineering feat had to be accomplished. This was the excavation of Sonning Cutting, nearly two miles long and 60 foot deep. Work had commenced in

Brunel's railway bridge across the Thames at Maidenhead.

The Royal County of Berkshire

Autumn 1836 but as the job had to be achieved by navvies working with spades the progress was slow. The geology was gravel and hardened clay, which was conducive to landslides in wet weather and often resulted in a morass of mud. Hundreds of men slaved for three years with wheelbarrows and horse-drawn trucks to form the Cutting and many fatal accidents occurred.

At one point during the excavations the workmen went on strike because there were no wages forthcoming. The navvies hung about the streets of Reading for several days and were brought to order by a squad of Horse Guards sent from Windsor. Many strikers were reduced to begging from the Reading townspeople, but finally they gathered in the Forbury at Reading where they were told by the mayor that they would receive their money with back pay. Early in 1839 it was reported that there were 700 thousand cubic yards of earth still to be removed, and this was achieved by the end of the year by 1,220 men, 196 horses and two locomotives.

A G.W.R. Broad Gauge train in Sonning Cutting.

On 14th March 1840, Brunel and the Directors of the line came down to Reading on a trial run, which they accomplished in 70 minutes; and two weeks later the line was opened to the public. Work continued and before the end of 1840 the line through Berkshire was completed. The line linking London to Bristol was opened in its entirety on 30th June, 1841. In Berkshire it passed through Pangbourne, Goring, Cholsey for Wallingford, Didcot and Steventon. This last village was placed on the map and it was considered the station for Oxford, whilst Didcot which for years had been a sleepy settlement now came to life as a railway town, expanding to meet the needs of the iron road. The station itself was quite large, especially after it became the junction for Oxford, and its engine sheds provided additional jobs for local workers.

Other lines followed rapidly and by 1847 the other main line from Reading through the Kennet Valley to Newbury and Hungerford was opened. The branch line from Reading to Basingstoke opened in the following year linking the County town with the Southern Railway. Other companies in the south east linked Ascot, Wokingham and Bracknell with Reading, turning the town into a massive railway junction with three stations and changing it from a busy market town into an expanding commercial and administrative centre.

Slough station was not opened until 1840 due to opposition from Eton College, who maintained that the railway was encouraging the students to 'sample the fleshpots in London', and it was not until 1848 that consent was given for a branch from Slough to Windsor.

The effect of the railway in Berkshire on other traffic was catastrophic. The hardest hit were perhaps the waterways who lost a lot of their commercial business. These included the Kennet and Avon Canal and the Wilts and Berks Canal, which ran through the Vale of the White Horse. By 1866 the Thames Commissioners were £90,000 in debt and lost control of the river to the Thames Conservators.

The last stage coach from London to Bristol ran in 1843. The once busy Bath Road which was used to holding up to 90 coaches per day, became a virtual backwater. Towns along its route which had catered for the needs of coach travellers found that they had many redundant properties and coaching inns dwindled in status to mere public houses. Toll bridges, as at Maidenhead, lost 80% of their

Victorian Expansion and the Railway

Reading Station.

The Locomotive 'ARGUS' c 1869.

The Royal County of Berkshire

A Victorian pump at Sonning.

income and were subject to subsidies from the railway for a few years, after which they had to fend for themselves. On the other side of the coin, the railway brought commuters into Berkshire and middle class entrepreneurs, who bought up old properties and turned them into businesses and shops. In the end one thing out-weighed the other, especially as the new middle class provided churches and schools that could be used by the whole community.

From early Victorian times the benefits of the railway system brought expansion to all the urban centres in Berkshire. The most significant was the county town of Reading which, of all the towns, was best sited. Many new industries began to emerge bringing with them a need for labour and additional housing. The town expanded in all directions reaching the outer villages of Woodley, Tilehurst, Caversham and Whitley.

One of the largest of the new businesses was John Sutton & Son, the seed merchant who in 1837 settled in premises to the east of the Market Place. Sutton's Seeds had a reputation for quality and reliability and after a period they were being despatched from Reading to destinations all over the world. Their Reading headquarters was later called The Royal Seed Establishment with the numerous buildings covering an area of six acres.

Huntley & Palmer's biscuit factory was another large employer and was started by Joseph Huntley in 1822 who opened a biscuit factory in London Street. Joseph hit upon the idea of packing the biscuits in tin boxes and persuaded his son to manufacture the tins, which resulted in the birth of the firm Huntley, Bourne and Stevens, whose decorative boxes were used to send biscuits all over the world. In 1841 Huntley went into business with George Palmer, a partnership that flourished so well that by 1846 the firm moved to the large premises in King's Road, taking over a factory built in 1841 for a silk manufacturer. By 1860 the firm was acknowledged as the largest biscuit factory in England producing over 100 varieties to cater for all tastes. By the turn of the century the Huntley & Palmers employees numbered over 5000.

Brick and tile making was another major industry in Reading, supplies of suitable clay being available near the Kennet. There were kilns at Katesgrove, Coley and Tilehurst. At

Victorian Expansion and the Railway

Katesgrove, the Waterloo and Rose kilns were still very active at the end of the 19th century, whilst at Coley two firms were making bricks, tiles and pottery. Samuel Wheeler moved from Coley in 1885 and founded Tilehurst Potteries at Kentwood Hill. Similarly S & E Collier, the brickmaker with the best reputation, moved from Coley to Grovelands in Lower Tilehurst. Collier's distinctive brickwork can be seen all over Reading, and the firm was amongst the leading British manufacturers before it ceased business in 1965.

At Reading the main line railways attracted a host of industries, and with them thousands of people searching employment. The town expanded, mainly with street after street of small terraced houses to accommodate the working classes, whilst other areas provided detached houses in spacious gardens for the professional classes. The prosperity of the town was marked by the number of buildings and monuments erected at the end of the 19th century. The Town Hall, designed by Alfred Waterhouse, was opened with much ceremony in 1876, and to this the Public Library, Museum and Art Gallery, paid for mainly by public subscription were added in 1883–4. Reading was granted County Borough status in 1888, giving it independence from the Berkshire County Council.

By the 19th century the cloth trade, which had been present in Newbury since the 15th century had begun to decline. Nevertheless, the Greenham mills were still in operation in 1811. The opening of the Kennet and Avon Canal made it possible to start new industries and iron foundries and boat building yards were amongst these. In addition to these the old industries such as the corn and malt mills and breweries continued to flourish.

The forerunner of all modern lifeboats was invented in 1816 by William Plenty and launched at West Mills. The GWR railway reached Newbury in 1847 when a branch line from Reading was opened. Later the Didcot to Southampton link was completed as far as Winchester in 1885, and a further line to Lambourn in 1898. To a limited extent the town enjoyed a new prosperity, and like Reading improved its municipal buildings at the end of

A steam train at Didcot Junction station.

An early scene at Lambourn railway station.

151

The Royal County of Berkshire

the Victorian era. A corn exchange was erected in 1862, and a new Cattle Market in 1873. Additions to the Town Hall were made in 1878, but the whole building was demolished in 1908, when the present Municipal Offices were erected. One of the most imposing buildings in the town is the Museum, formerly the Cloth Hall, when the weaving industry was at its height.

Hungerford, being further west was one of those towns that did not expand to any degree during the Victorian era. The opening of the Kennet and Avon, like Newbury, brought some activity in 1810. In addition to being a market town, Hungerford became a point of despatch for materials travelling by canal. The wharf was busy loading gravel, chalk and whiting to the west, and timber to the east. In 1818 over 200 boats were using the canal and many stopped at the town to load and unload. When the main line railway opened in 1847 the expected prosperity never materialised, and many used the line to travel to bigger towns where jobs were more plentiful.

Most building during this period was confined to churches. However, a new Corn Exchange, was opened in October 1871, the market element still being strong. In order to provide some employment in the town two engineering firms sprung up the first being Catrell & Co at the Eddington Iron Works. The other was the competitive business provided by Henry Gibbons at the Kennet Works. To a limited extent this helped the economy of the town.

The 19th century growth was more pronounced in the urban centres east of Reading. Being close to London, with better rail service, the effect was greater. Windsor, which has always been dependent on the Castle and the resultant tourists, for its livelihood, developed little from the industrial point of view. And yet there was considerable growth in the population as more people decided to live in the area. The census records that the inhabitants increased from 3,197 in 1801 to 7,528 in 1841 after Victoria had ascended the throne. But a report at this time showed that out of the 2,500 acres of agricultural land in the Borough 1,700 of them were in the possession of the Crown and could in no way be developed. The expansion of the town was confined to the erection of houses for the gentry, the traders and the poor with many elaborate structures to fall in line with

---

S. & E. COLLIER,
MANUFACTURERS OF THE CELEBRATED
READING RED TILES.

SPECIALITIES.
Red Tiles for Weather Tiling & Roofing, including Hip & Valley Tiles, Angle Tiles, Sprocket Tiles, Gable Tiles, & Tiles for Undereaves.

RIDGE TILES.
Ridge Tile Finials, Terminals, & Intersections Pier Balls, Air Bricks, & Mural Tiles.

Plain & Ornamental
RED CHIMNEY POTS.
Agricultural Butt Joint Pipes of all sizes.
Red Socket Pipes for Agricultural purposes.
Architects' designs worked out with care.

RED GARDEN EDGING TILES.
All kinds of Garden Pottery, also Orchid Po and Fancy Flower Pots.

TELEGRAPHIC ADDRESS: "COLLIER, READING."

Victorian Expansion and the Railway

fashionable requirements.

Before the coming of the railway Maidenhead was one long street of premises associated with the coaching era. Due to its close proximity to London, middle class entrepreneurs moved in and turned the High Street into a shopping area with many fashionable stores. The population grew quickly and so did the town. By 1875 Queen Street and King Street had been constructed with many other linking roads, bringing new shops and businesses. Fashionable villas sprung up on Castle Hill and in Norfolk Park to accommodate the new traders and roads of terraced houses for the working classes. Many new churches and schools were built that previously had not been considered as a requirement.

The biggest change however took place in the area of the riverside. The new railway had brought hoards of excursionists, playboys and debutantes to the Thames which hitherto had been a working river. There were pageants, regattas and other aquatic sports which culminated in a parade of boats at Boulter's Lock on Ascot Sunday. Boats and boathouses were built to satisfy the demands of visitors, together with new hotels to accommodate weekenders. Many dubious clubs were built along the river banks and Maidenhead gained the reputation that Brighton had at a later date. "Are you married, or do you live in Maidenhead?" people would ask. King Edward VII would regularly dine at Skindles Hotel, when spending weekends at Taplow Court or Cliveden.

The two east Berkshire towns which had never had the benefit of a river for communication were Wokingham and Bracknell. Before the railway reached them in 1849 they were not considered the most prosperous of towns. In fact Bracknell was little more than a large village and only expanded in size from 1948, when it was considered as a site of a 'new town'. Today, it has one of the largest industrial areas in the County. It stands on an area of acid soils which are totally unsuitable for agricultural purposes, but there are pockets of clay useful in brickmaking.

A Miles M2 Hawk at Woodley Aerodrome c 1933.

The Royal County of Berkshire

For nearly 700 years Wokingham remained a small town serving a mainly rural community. Amongst its main industries were sack and leather factories, the latter being produced at many sites in the town, most of them close to the Emmbrook stream. From around 1850 a small industrial site grew up near the Emmbrook and the local brickmaking industry began to expand with the railway providing easy transport for heavy materials. One of the fields was in Oxford Road and another at the Blue Pool site, which for many years had its own railway connections.

GREAT WESTERN RAILWAY.
LONDON TO MAIDENHEAD AND TWYFORD.
(OPENED JULY 1, 1839.)

CHAPTER 15
The Post-1974 Additions

In 1974 the shape of Berkshire changed with the new Government regulations. The familiar boot-shaped outline disappeared as a large portion of the north-western section was appended to Oxfordshire. This was considered most unfortunate for historians who saw the loss of the White Horse at Uffington plus the two original county towns of Wallingford and Abingdon as well as Alfred's birthplace of Wantage. In exchange for this loss the county gained land at the eastern end from Buckinghamshire which included the towns of Slough and Eton and a series of small villages.

People can perhaps be forgiven for thinking that Slough has no history and that it evolved in the twentieth century as one large industrial site populated by immigrants who came to the area looking for work. To a certain extent this is true but under the commercial facade the town dates back to Saxon times and the name Slough appears in records as early as 1196 when it was spelt "Slo". In Shakespeare's "Merry Wives of Windsor", Bardolph is heard to say "as soon as I came beyond Eton they threw me off… in a slough of mire", indicating the state of the land in the 16th century.

The oldest parts of the town are Upton and Chalvey, and there are still other ancient peripheral settlements that remain in Bucks. Upton is mentioned in the Domesday Book as Opetone, and was land of the King belonging in Saxon times to Earl Harold. It was an area of 18 hides with a population of roughly 100 people, a mill and a fishery. The church of St Laurence at Upton still retains some Norman features and was the centre of the manor. Immediately behind the church is Upton Court, recently restored, and dated by tree ring

The Royal County of Berkshire

Slough High Street c 1880.

Upton Church in 1825.

St Laurence's Church Upton-cum-Chalvey, 19th century.

dating to 1325 A.D., making it perhaps the oldest secular building in Berkshire.

The nave and tower of the present church were built about 1100 and the nave lengthened and the chancel added about 1160 after Upton Manor passed to the Augustinan Canons of Merton Priory in Surrey in 1156. The Priory held the manor until the Dissolution in 1538, a riverside portion of which was levied to Henry VI in 1443 for the endowment of Eton College, which will be mentioned later.

The settlement was later known as Upton-cum-Chalvey. The earliest record of Chalvey. usually interpreted as "Calves Island", was in 1217 but it is possible that it was part of Upton at Domesday, perhaps pasture land for cattle. The manor of Chalvey came into the possession of Richard Bulstrode in 1496, who died in 1502 "seised of lands held of Merton Priory, and of Chalvey Manor and Upton". This is presumably why there are so many brasses of the Bulstrode family in Upton church.

There are few early references of Slough as a settlement, although an important mention is made on 23rd April, 1442, when Henry VI placed an order for bricks to be made for the building of Eton College. Nearly 2½ million were eventually supplied between the years 1442 and 1551 at 10 pence a thousand. It was the introduction of coaches and the Eton Montem ceremony that originally put Slough on the map. The town started as a few buildings situated at the Crown crossroads and developed as traffic increased on the Bath Road. At the peak period there were 77 stage coaches, 105 post chaises and 80 stage wagons passing through every day. The Crown was the largest of the posting houses at Slough with the Castle and Windmill Hotel at Salt Hill receiving more attention during the 18th century.

The area of Salt Hill, now firmly part of Slough and close to the Town Hall, was once a separate settlement on the border of the parishes of Upton-cum-Chalvey and Farnham Royal. Camden's map of 1675 shows a mill standing on a site near to the Windmill Hotel and the Domesday Book records a mill, which would be powered by water on Chalvey Brook.

The Post-1974 Additions

The Royal County of Berkshire

The Montem Mound at Salt Hill is a curiosity and provides the origin of the name "Salt". The mound itself stands next to the Bath Road, and has recently been renovated. During renovation some Norman pottery was found which may indicate that it was at one time a motte to a small castle. Its fame, however, comes from its use by the Eton College boys. The origins are obscure but it is said that the Eton boys were marched to Salt Hill daily to play, but by the reign of Henry VIII they had acquired the playing fields by the college. The old custom was then celebrated annually as a commemoration.

The earliest account of the Montem ceremony was compiled about 1561 by the headmaster William Malin, who described it as an initiation for new boys. It then became a ritual for collecting "salt" or money as a contribution towards the expenses of the senior collegers who went to King's College, Cambridge. This later developed into a full scale dress occasion when the whole school was mustered in semi-military array, with a band and colours. Many, including royalty, attended the ceremony and made generous donations. The last celebration was in 1844 when Prince Albert contributed £100 to the funds.

The history of Slough cannot be told without mention of the Trading Estate, the first of its kind in the world. This was opened in 1925 and was formed from the so called 'Slough Dump' which was a Motor Repair Depot at the end of the first World War. Many of the factories that operated there, like Mars and Aspro, are now household names. It was presumably the heavy industrial activity that prompted Sir John Betjeman to write "come friendly bombs and rain on Slough", a line of his poem which he later regretted writing.

The Montem Mound, Slough.

Just as the town of Windsor grew up around the Castle, so the neighbouring parish of Eton grew up around its famous College. Linked to Windsor by a bridge across the Thames, the small town of Eton comprises a long narrow High Street which once formed part of the main road to London. By the 13th century the town had reached its present limits as the Hundred Rolls for 1275–6 refer to the "village of Eton from Baldewin Bridge to Windsor Bridge" and these landmarks define the area between the College and Windsor.

The Post-1974 Additions

The early name Eyton indicates a settlement located on an island, and the land towards Eton Wick which comprised many seasonal meadows in medieval times, substantiates this. A second bridge across the water when leaving Eton en route for Slough was Beggar's Bridge, which was always falling down as in 1302 when it was declared a danger to travellers. It was superseded by a stone bridge in 1443 when it was required to bear the weight of the numerous loads of bricks transported for the building of the College.

Before the Conquest the manor of Eton was held by Queen Edith and at the time of the Domesday Survey by Walter FitzOther, the warden of the Windsor forests and Constable of Windsor Castle. Walter was an ancestor of the family of Windsor and his son, who inherited the manor at a later date, took on the name of William de Windsor.

It was in the year 1440 that Henry VI founded the King's College of Our Lady of Eton beside Windsor and a year later King's College, Cambridge, which was to be supplied with scholars from Eton. The foundation was to include a community of secular priests, 10 of whom were Fellows, a pilgrimage church and an almshouse. Seventy scholars were to receive free education.

Henry endowed the College with a substantial income from land, and leased from the Prior of Merton a large portion of the manor of Upton with a mill and fisheries which abutted the Thames. The licence for alienation of the land was dated 5th June 1443 and it was described as follows:

"a weir on the river Thames at Upton, county Buckingham of old called Bullokeslok, with the fishery and waters thereto pertaining, to wit, from the east corner of the land or close called 'le werde' on the west side to the fishery in the river called 'Cokkeshole' on the east side with four eyots (islands) and all those lands, meadows, feeding grounds, pastures with torrents...enclosed and lying by Eton between the Thames on the east and the way leading from New Wyndesore towards 'le slough', on the west between 'le werde' on the south and the way leading from 'spitelbrigge' (Beggar's Bridge) to Datchet on the north, and extending by the bank of the Thames from 'le werde' forty feet beyond. 'Cowpennyng' on the east...in exchange for 100 shillings yearly which the Abbot of Reading renders to

An Eton boy in 1860.

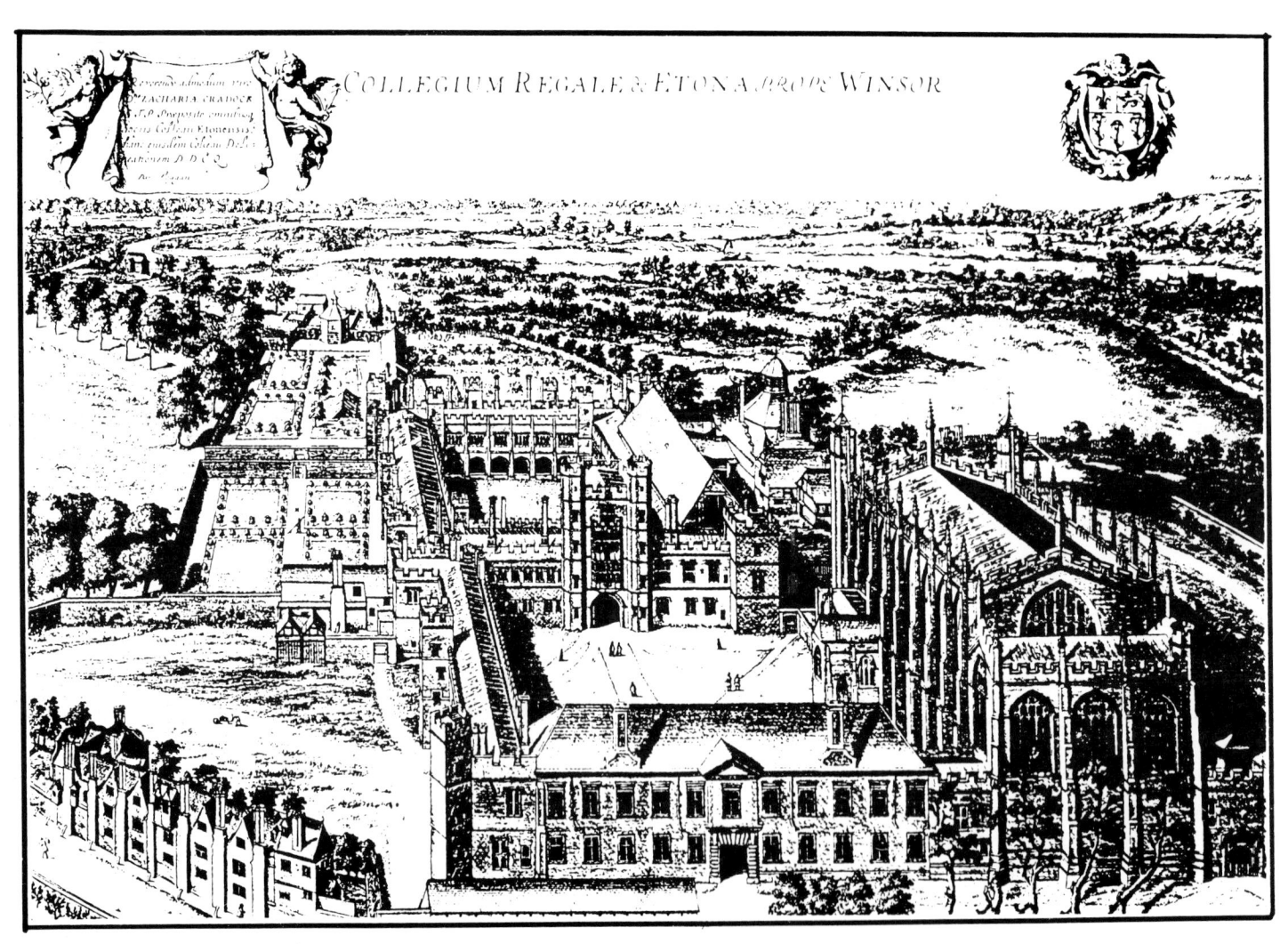

View of Eton College in 1865.

the Provost and College from a yearly farm for lands in Esthenrith, county Berks of the King's grant. License also for the Provost and College to grant the said rent to the Prior and convent."

Henry took a personal interest in the building which led to frequent changes of plan. In 1448 he had the partially constructed church demolished to make way for another on a grander scale. The accommodation block along the north side of School Yard was completed in 1443 and by 1450 the Lower School, Long Chamber, College Hall and Cloister Court were in use.

By 1470 the Chapel was still not finished, but a former Provost of Eton, Bishop Waynflete came to the rescue and had the choir roofed in wood and added an antichapel at the west end. This work was completed by 1482 and is the Chapel that we see today built in Perpendicular Gothic style. Lupton's Tower, and the range within which it is incorporated was built in 1520 by Henry Redman, and the similarity with Redman's work at Hampton Court is notable.

Numerous other buildings including a library and extensive accommodation have been built in Eton as part of the College complex. The initial 70 scholars for which Henry provided has now increased to 1,250 with 135 masters. The school has produced many famous men including writers Gray, Shelley, Aldous Huxley and George Orwell. The Duke of Wellington, of Waterloo fame, studied at Eton as did twenty other Prime Ministers, ranging from Walpole and Pitt the Elder, to MacMillan and Douglas-Home. The College continues its tradition today and retains its position as perhaps the most famous school in the world.

The village of Datchet is situated across the Thames from Windsor Castle, the river being spanned by the Victoria and Albert bridges, built of iron girders. At one time the short route from London to Windsor Castle was via the ferry at Datchet and was frequently used by royal personages. During the 16th century many payments from the privy purse have been recorded to the ferryman. The ferry was discontinued in 1706 when a bridge free of toll was erected, this being replaced in 1770 by a wooden structure on stone piers. Another

The Post-1974 Additions

The Electric Telegraph Cottage at Slough.

The Royal County of Berkshire

curious bridge, half wood and half iron, was erected in 1811 but this was replaced by the Victoria Bridge in 1851.

The first mention of Datchet occurs between 990 and 994 when King Ethelred granted some land there. By Domesday it was in the hands of Giles de Pinkney, as was Maidenhead and Boveney further up the Thames. The village seems to have grown up around the church which was entirely rebuilt in 1857. The manor house which was opposite the church was a 16th century building close by the Royal Stag Inn built one century later.

The Domesday site of Ditton lies to the north of the parish where Ditton House now stands. When sub-infeudation occurred in the area the manor of Riding was closely associated with Ditton. Another manor, Datchet St Helen, was owned by the priory of St Helens, Bishopsgate. From a dispute over a meadow there is evidence to show that the priory owned lands in Datchet in 1263.

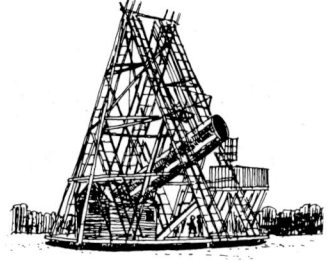

The adjoining parish of Horton is ostensibly an ancient parish fed by tributories of the Thames and Colne. However today it has little to show of an ancient nature and three moated sites in the area have now been virtually obliterated in the name of progress. Even the church of St Michael, erected in the 12th century, was severely re-modelled in 1875. The most interesting feature is the annexed Romany graveyard where the stones are immaculate and flowers in bloom can be seen throughout the year.

Sir William Herschel's Telescope in Slough.

It was, however, mentioned in the Domesday Book as belonging like Eton to the Constable of Windsor Castle, Walter FitzOther. Later Horton Manor was broken up into Berkin Manor, Okhide and Speelings probably represented by the three moated sites.

The last of the newly acquired Berkshire settlements is the village of Wraysbury which was held by Robert Gernon in 1086. Edmund, one of the King's thegns held it before the Conquest, when, as the Domesday Book tells us the manor supplied "hay for the cattle of the court" in Old Windsor. Substantial remains of the Saxon settlement have been excavated in recent years, revealing the humble dwellings of the serfs who slaved away for the King. No doubt some of the produce from the two mills and four fisheries mentioned at Domesday also turned up on the dining table at the royal palace.

On the Ankerwycke estate lies the ruins of a priory of Benedictine Nuns, founded around 1160 by Gilbert de Muntfichet. The first prioress is given as Lettice in 1194. The priory, which had 6 nuns, was endowed with land at Henley and Windsor, as well as Egham in Surrey and Greenford and Stanwell in Middlesex. In addition King Henry III in 1242 granted the nuns license to pasture sixty pigs every year in Windsor Forest. Very little is known of the history of this priory which at the Dissolution was granted by the King for the foundation of the later short-lived abbey at Bisham.

Near the ruins of the nunnery is a large yew tree traditionally associated with a meeting between Henry VIII and Anne Boleyn, and close by is Magna Carta Island in the Thames, where a preserved stone is said to be the site where the great document was signed by King John. This story, however, conflicts with the other suggested site on Runnymede meadows.

Other buildings of interest in the parish include the 17th century George Inn and Place Farm, which is popularly known as King John's Hunting Lodge.

The Post-1974 Additions

Observatory House, Windsor Road, Slough.

The Yew Tree at Ankerwyke Priory, Wraysbury.

Slough Station in 1843.

The Royal County of Berkshire

Unitary Authorities

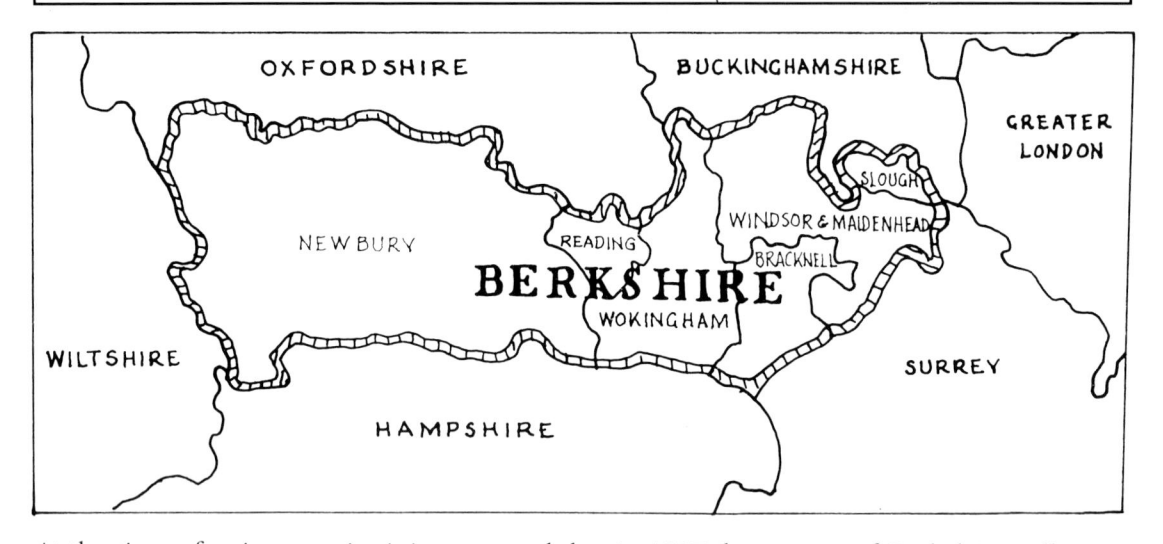

At the time of going to print it is proposed that in 1997 the county of Berkshire will come under the administration of six unitary authorities and that the County Council will be abolished. By far the biggest authority will be Newbury which will encompass Hungerford and all the downland settlements. In the more densely populated eastern half, which includes all the other major towns and their associated industries, the districts tend to be smaller. This plan might be affected by future legislation, but an assurance has been made that Berkshire will not lose its identity as a county. The present population of Berkshire is 761,000 people.

Index to Selected People and Places

A
Abingdon 10, 20, 41, 42, 43, 57, 105, 110, 138
Abingdon Abbey 39, 58, 93, 100
Albert, Prince 76
Aldermaston 54
Alfred, King 9, 10, 36, 59, 75, 85
Ankerwyke Priory 66
Anne of Cleves 66
Anne, Queen 119, 123
Ardington 88
Ascot 123, 147
Ascot Races 123, 125
Ashbury 10, 20
Aston 62
Austin Canons 57
Avington 100

B
Basildon 17
Bath 133
Bath Road 120, 133, 134
Belgae 23, 25
Benedictines 41, 57, 69
Berrocshire 9
Bisham Abbey 66, 67
Blewbury 13, 62, 88
Bracknell 14, 32, 121, 153
Bray 12, 20, 32, 36, 109, 128, 130
Brightwalton 88, 109
Brightwell 88
Brimpton 115
Bristol 42, 83, 133, 143
Bromhall Priory 65
Bronze Age 19, 20
Brunel Bridge 144, 145
Brunel, I.K. 143, 146
Bucklebury 36
Bull-Baiting 120, 121

C
Camlet Way 30
Caversham 17, 32, 69, 114, 116
Chaddleworth 88
Challow 9
Chalvey 155, 157
Charles I 116, 117
Chieveley 88
Childrey 87
Cholsey 62, 146
Cissa 57
Clewer 71, 128
Cluniacs 62
Cock-fighting 120, 121
Cole, River 12
Compton 119
Cookham 22, 29, 30, 36, 55, 109, 128
Cox Green Villa 31
Cricket 130

D
Datchet 126, 133, 161, 162
Devil's Highway 12, 133
Didcot 12, 88, 146, 150
Ditton 162
Domesday 38, 41, 51, 54, 86, 93, 99, 162
Donnington Castle 115, 116
Dorchester-on-Thames 29, 35

165

E
East Hannay 88
East Hendred 88, 89
East Ilsley 79, 93, 102
Edward the Confessor 38, 39, 45, 55, 59, 63, 71, 119
Edward I 74, 82
Edward III 72, 78, 82
Edward IV 72, 74, 83
Edward VI 78
Edward VII 76
Elizabeth I 68, 81, 104
Elizabeth II 76
Emmbrook 154
Ethelred the Unready 36
Eton 20, 76, 128, 158, 159
Eton College 128, 159, 160

F
Faringdon 86, 87, 100, 101
Finchampstead 23
Fitzcount, Brian 41
Football 130
Frilford 36
Fulmer 34
Furze Platt 18

G
George VI 76
Gloucester 41
Gooch, Daniel 143, 144
Goosey 10, 87
Great Coxwell 127

Great Western Railway 143, 144
Greenham 54, 168
Greenham Common 115
Greyfriars 69
Grimsdyke 88

H
Hampstead Marshal 115
Hampstead Norris 93
Harold, Earl 39
Hean 42, 57, 59
Hedgerley 34
Henley 55, 114, 126
Henry I 45, 54, 62, 72
Henry II 62, 72
Henry III 54
Henry VI 82, 100, 159
Henry VIII 72, 81, 103, 119, 163
Holyport 18, 35
Hungerford 9, 12, 53, 54, 100, 114, 136, 152
Huntley & Palmer 148
Hurley 122, 135
Hurley Priory 62, 63, 64
Hurst 39

I
Inkpen 10, 12
Iron Age 22, 23, 24, 26

J
Jack of Newbury 100, 103

James I 119
John, King 9, 72, 163

K
Kennet, River 12, 35, 51, 111, 140
Kennet & Avon Canal 12, 42, 141, 143, 147, 149
Kingsbury 72
Kingston Lisle 87
Kintbury 36, 53, 85, 115
Knowl Hill 25

L
Lambourn 22, 66, 86, 87, 123, 149, 151
Lambourn, River 12
Letcombe Bassett 87
Littlecote 33
Loddon, River 12, 18, 55, 111
London 41, 42, 111, 133, 143

M
Magna Carta 72, 74, 163
Maidenhead 14, 25, 31, 49, 56, 83, 84, 116, 126, 134, 142, 143, 153
Mandevelle, Geoffrey de 63
Mesolithic 18, 20
Midgham 54
Montem 158
Mortimer 22
Motorway M4 12
Moulsford 64

N
Neolithic 19, 20
Newbury 12, 29, 51, 52, 53, 82, 85, 100, 104, 105, 106, 111, 115, 123, 139, 149

O
Ock, River 10, 12
Offa, King 57, 87
Oxford 42, 59, 111, 137, 146

P
Paleolithic 17
Pang, River 93
Pangbourne 29, 146

R
Reading 14, 35, 42, 44, 45, 46, 57, 80, 81, 100, 104, 110, 113, 114, 124, 126, 135, 146, 147, 149
Reading Abbey 60, 61, 62, 137
Reading Gaol 110
Remenham 63, 120, 126
Robin Hood's Arbour 25
Runnymede 10, 20

S
Sandalford Priory 68
St. George's Chapel 76
Sandhurst 10, 78
Shakespeare 155
Shaw House 115
Shillingford 87
Shottesbrooke 69
Shrivenham 10, 87
Silchester 25, 27, 28
Slough 14, 35, 147, 155, 157, 158, 161
Sonning Cutting 144, 146
Sparsholt 87
Speen 103, 142
Speenhamland 109, 135, 136
Staines 12, 29
Stevens, Joseph 18
Steventon 12
Streatley 70
Sutton Courtney 88
Sutton, John 148
Sulhamstead 140

T
Thames, River 10, 71, 111, 126, 137
Thatcham 18, 29, 54
Treacher, Llewellyn 18
Twyford 39, 111, 120, 144, 154

U
Uffington 12, 23, 34, 87
Upton 155, 156, 157

V
Victoria, Queen 74, 76, 96

W
Wallingford 10, 39, 40, 41, 42, 59, 64, 105, 113
Waltham St. Lawrence 30, 63
Wantage 10, 37, 85, 86, 100, 121, 123
Wargrave 54, 55, 111, 120, 129
Wawcott 18
Wayland's Smithy 20, 21
Wessex 36
West Hannay 87
Westminster Abbey 71
Whistley 38
White Horse 10, 16, 25, 87, 155
White Waltham 36, 63
Wickham 88
Windsor 10, 14, 39, 45, 47, 48, 50, 71–78, 82, 111, 112, 121, 123
Windsor Castle 10, 65, 73, 74, 112, 117
Windsor Forest 93, 94, 95, 96
Winkfield 93
William I 38, 39, 71, 93
Wittenham, Long 23, 88
Woolhampton 98
Woolstone 32
Wokingham 14, 51, 111, 121, 129, 153, 154
Wraysbury 74, 162, 163
Wytham Wood 98

Y
Yattendon 93

Radley College